LEGENDS OF
INDIA

Vishwamitra Sharma

V&S PUBLISHERS

Published by:

V&S PUBLISHERS

F-2/16, Ansari road, Daryaganj, New Delhi-110002
☎ 23240026, 23240027 • *Fax:* 011-23240028
Email: info@vspublishers.com • *Website:* www.vspublishers.com

Regional Office : Hyderabad
5-1-707/1, Brij Bhawan (Beside Central Bank of India Lane)
Bank Street, Koti, Hyderabad - 500 095
☎ 040-24737290
E-mail: vspublishershyd@gmail.com

Branch Office : Mumbai
Jaywant Industrial Estate, 1st Floor–108, Tardeo Road
Opposite Sobo Central Mall, Mumbai – 400 034
☎ 022-23510736
E-mail: vspublishersmum@gmail.com

Follow us on:

DISCLAIMER

While every attempt has been made to provide accurate and timely information in this book, neither the author nor the publisher assumes any responsibility for errors, unintended omissions or commissions detected therein. The author and publisher make no representation or warranty with respect to the comprehensiveness or completeness of the contents provided.

All matters included have been simplified under professional guidance for general information only without any warranty for applicability on an individual. Any mention of an organization or a website in the book by way of citation or as a source of additional information doesn't imply the endorsement of the content either by the author or the publisher. It is possible that websites cited may have changed or removed between the time of editing and publishing the book.

Results from using the expert opinion in this book will be totally dependent on individual circumstances and factors beyond the control of the author and the publisher.

It makes sense to elicit advice from well informed sources before implementing the ideas given in the book. The reader assumes full responsibility for the consequences arising out from reading this book. For proper guidance, it is advisable to read the book under the watchful eyes of parents/guardian. The purchaser of this book assumes all responsibility for the use of given materials and information. The copyright of the entire content of this book rests with the author/publisher. Any infringement/ transmission of the cover design, text or illustrations, in any form, by any means, by any entity will invite legal action and be responsible for consequences thereon.

Printed at Repro Knowledgecast Limited, Thane

Contents

FREEDOM FIGHTERS & STATESMEN

POLITICAL LEADERS

SOCIAL REFORMERS

Preface

Undoubtedly the cradle of the first major civilisation, five millennia ago India was a fabled land where milk and honey flowed freely. Through the next few millennia, the land produced many noble souls who kept the country's rich spiritual and cultural heritage throbbing. From astronomy, mathematics and medicine to spiritual mastery and renowned universities, the land produced the best in all spheres.

Somewhere down the line, we lost our way, with complacency and inertia taking over, even as the world forged ahead and we were enslaved by different foreign invaders, including the British.

Centuries of serfdom, strife and struggle followed, as we sought to assert our identity and preserve the nation's rich cultural heritage. It was during this period of enslavement that countless inspiring personalities came to the helm, exhorting countrymen to awake from their slumber, throw off the foreign yoke and reclaim India's rightful place among the comity of nations. One man who inspired Indians and foreigners through his oratory was 19th Century legend, Swami Vivekananda, who once said: "First reform yourself before you reform the world."

Some of the most inspiring personalities lived during the 20th Century, a crucial period in the country's march towards independence. In this reawakening, individuals from every sphere contributed their mite: freedom fighters, politicians, social reformers.

Added to these were the inspiring examples of Gandhi, Tilak, Vinoba Bhave, Sri Aurobindo, Rabindranath Tagore and countless others who led from the front during the freedom struggle. Most Indian leaders eschewed violence, focusing on our ancient tradition of non-violent protest.

In this amazing turnaround, hundreds and thousands of Indians have played a key role. Selecting only few names has been an arduous task, with other equally deserving ones having been left out due to space constraints. This is not just a collection of achievements and milestones by select individuals – it is the story of an entire era.

I am grateful to M/s V&S Publishers for accepting this book for publication. Thanks also to Ms A Sunita Purushottaman for helping me in this endeavour. And grateful thanks to the editorial staff without whose untiring efforts this book would not have seen the light of day.

–**Vishwamitra Sharma**
C-3/58, Lawrence Road
Delhi – 110 035
Tel: 27194317

Freedom Fighters & Statesmen

Mahatma Gandhi

Personality of the Millennium

(1869–1948)

Mahatma Gandhi shared the same disposition as Lord Rama, Lord Krishna, Jesus and Ashoka. In the entire 20th Century, there was none who could belittle Mahatma Gandhi's towering personality. But just as all luminaries come to earth with a purpose, Gandhiji came with the purpose of securing independence for India. It's a pity that though he delivered us from the bonds of servitude, he did not have the opportunity to enjoy the moments of glory. His dream of a united and strong India could not be fulfilled. It's ironical that Gandhiji did not live long enough to see the country stride on the path to progress. The simple man that he was, his immense charisma drew not only the rich towards him, but even inspired the poor.

There is no denying the fact that Mahatma Gandhi is the *personality of the millennium.* Gandhiji was born on 2 October 1869 at Porbandar, Gujarat. His father, Karamchand Gandhi, was the *diwan* (chief minister) of Porbandar. He was not a highly qualified person, but was a good administrator and knew his job well. Gandhiji's mother, Putlibai, was a deeply religious lady and she influenced him a lot. It was her piety and truthfulness that made him forsake and oppose vice. He would readily accept it if he committed any wrong. Gandhiji was brought up on the religious tenets of *Vaishnavism* (worship of Lord Vishnu) and Jainism. Both the faiths advocated the principles of *ahimsa* or non-injury to all living beings. So he was brought up on the principles of non-violence, vegetarianism and tolerance.

Gandhiji was an average student at school. Like every normal child, he had his share of childhood and adolescent escapades. But he resolved never to commit such transgressions and tried to improve himself. At the age of 13, he was married to Kasturba.

In 1887, he was just able to clear his matriculation from the University of Bombay. Then he joined Samaldas College in Bhaunagar (now Bhavnagar). He was not happy in college because he had to take up English instead of Gujarati. So when his family gave him the proposal of going to England to study law, he jumped at it. Thereafter, he sailed to "a land of philosophers and poets, the very centre of civilisation" in September 1888 and joined the Inner Temple, one of the four London law colleges. He took up English and Latin earnestly but it was difficult for him to adjust to Western society, especially because of his vegetarianism. But he met people like Edward Carpenter, GB Shaw and Annie Besant, idealists who were instrumental in shaping his personality and inspiring him to take up the role of leading the freedom struggle in India.

His mother died while he was in England. When he returned to India in July 1891, he tried to start his practice in Bombay, but failed to make a mark. So he moved to Rajkot and took up the job of drafting petitions for litigants. It was during this time that he had the opportunity of going to South Africa on a year's contract from an Indian company which was based in Natal, South Africa. It was there that he first saw how the coloured people were subjected to inhuman treatment by the white government. In one instance, when he was travelling to Pretoria, he was thrown out of a first-class railway compartment along with his baggage because he dared to occupy a compartment reserved for whites only. This incident led him to revolt against such inhuman practices and made him determined not to accept injustice and indignity.

Gandhiji tried to educate the people about their rights and duties. However, he had to sail back to India after the lapse of the contract in June 1894. He asked the people to protest against a bill that was to be introduced in the Natal Legislative Assembly to deny Indians the right to vote. The people saw a leader in Gandhiji, so they requested him to stay back. Gandhiji was never interested in politics and was afraid of public speaking. But the July of 1894 saw him metamorphose into an active political campaigner. He was just 25 then. Although he was not able to prevent the passage of the bill, he was able to organise a lot of support and got noticed by the press in Natal, India and England. The same year he founded the Natal Indian Congress to bring the Indian community under one banner. *The Times* of London and the *Statesman* and *Englishman* of Calcutta voiced grievances of the Natal Indians.

In 1896 he returned to India to take his wife and children to South Africa. On his return to Durban in January 1897, he was attacked by a white mob. When the question of punishing the guilty came up, Gandhiji refused to prosecute the wrong doers.

On the outbreak of the Boer War in South Africa in 1899, he raised a body of volunteers which included barristers, accountants, artisans and labourers. But his contribution was not recognised by the Europeans in South Africa. In 1906, the Transvaal Government introduced an ordinance that was particularly insulting to the Indian population. Gandhiji organised a mass rally in protest against the ordinance at Johannesburg in September 1906 and vowed to defy the ordinance and to accept any punishment. Thus was born *satyagraha* (appeal to truth). His struggle in South Africa lasted more than seven years. The Indian community too willingly supported Gandhiji and was not deterred from taking part in the struggle by the atrocities of the British. The end of the struggle came when the Governments of India and Britain intervened and the South African Government accepted a compromise.

Because of his activities in South Africa, not only was he a known figure in India but also familiar with the people in other British colonies. When he returned to India in 1915, he was acclaimed as an esteemed leader. The elite business class of India had formed an organisation called the Congress and they did not have any agenda except petitioning the British Government. Gandhiji's experiment with satyagraha in South Africa gave a new impetus to the freedom struggle in India. When he returned to India, not only leaders, even the Indian people welcomed him with open arms. The Indians found in Gandhiji a leader who acted as a buoy and harnessed the strength of the people for the independence struggle. But, his struggle for freedom in India was different from that in South Africa.

People of the whole country, irrespective of caste, creed and religion, became involved in Gandhiji's freedom struggle. With the Champaran, Rowlatt Act and the Khilafat Movements, he was able to involve the people from all over India and thus became the unrivalled leader of the Congress. His position in the Indian struggle was similar to the position occupied by Lord Krishna in the Mahabharata war. Even without wielding a weapon, the Lord steered the Pandavas to victory. Gandhiji was initially not a member of the Congress, but he became its lifeline.

After returning to India, Gandhiji met Indian leaders like Sir Pherozeshah Mehta, Lokmanya Tilak and Gokhale and toured the nation. His first satyagraha revolution was at Champaran in Bihar where the farmers were forced to cultivate indigo for the British. It was here that he met prominent leaders of Bihar like Rajendra Prasad and they also pledged their support to Gandhiji.

In August 1919, he stirred a nation-wide protest against the Rowlatt Act, which gave the British the authority to imprison without trial. Gandhiji launched a satyagraha and people all over the country participated in his struggle. In the spring of 1919 a gathering of around 4,000 people, who had collected for a meeting at Jallianwala Bagh in Amritsar, were fired upon by soldiers and several hundreds were killed. The whole nation was rocked by the incident and Gandhiji decided to call off the struggle.

By 1920, Gandhiji became a prominent national leader. He believed that it was because of our weakness that we were being ruled by the British. He launched the Non-cooperation Movement where he asked students to boycott government-aided schools and colleges and told people to leave government service. The response was overwhelming. In spite of large-scale arrests, the movement picked up. In February 1922, a violent mob set fire to a police station in Chauri Chaura killing 22 policemen. Gandhiji decided to call off the movement. He was arrested in March 1922 but was released in 1924 because of ill health.

Meanwhile, disunity between the Hindus and Muslims had crept in. Gandhiji tried to persuade the two communities to forsake their fanaticism. There was a serious communal outbreak.

11

Gandhiji then undertook a three-week fast in 1924 to arouse the people to follow the path of non-violence.

In 1927, the British Government appointed Sir John Simon to head a constitutional reform commission. The Congress and other parties boycotted the commission because it did not contain any Indian member. In 1928, Gandhiji demanded Dominion status for India at the Calcutta Congress meeting. In March 1930, he launched the Dandi March in protest against the imposition of tax on salt. Around 60,000 people were imprisoned in the nation-wide non-violent strike against the British.

In 1931, after talks with Lord Irwin, he called off the strike and agreed to go to England to attend the Round Table Conference. The conference was a great disappointment because it concentrated on the plight of the minority communities in India rather than the issue of transfer of power to the Indians.

Back in India, Lord Willingdon succeeded Lord Irwin. The new British viceroy tried to curb the growing influence of Gandhiji, who was imprisoned. In September 1932, he undertook a fast to protest against the attempt of the British to segregate the "untouchables" by allotting them separate electorates in the new constitution. A mass campaign was launched to stop discrimination against the "untouchables". Gandhiji called them "Harijans" (the children of God).

In 1934, he resigned from the leadership and membership of the Congress. He felt that the members had adopted the policy of non-violence for political reasons. He went to Sevagram, a village in central India, and concentrated on the uplift of weaker sections of society.

In 1939, the Second World War broke out. It was a crucial phase in India's independence struggle. Gandhiji wanted the British to withdraw from India. Gandhiji launched a massive campaign called the 'Quit India' Movement. There were violent outbreaks and an attempt was made to curb the movement.

The war ended in 1945 and the elections that ensued in Britain were won by the Labour Party. They decided to grant independence to India but the Muslim League wanted a separate state for themselves. Tripartite negotiations were held for the next two years between the Congress Party, the Muslim League and the British Government. In mid-August, there came a breakthrough in the talks when it was decided to partition India to form the Muslim state of Pakistan. With Partition came the mass exodus and massacre of innocent people on both sides.

Even before the negotiations were on, there was large-scale communal violence. The incidents pained Gandhiji. He immersed himself in the task of healing the scars inflicted by communal conflicts. In Calcutta and Delhi he was able to bring about communal truce.

Gandhiji used to organise prayer sessions. On 30 January 1948, when Gandhiji was being led to the prayer hall at Birla House in Delhi, he was assassinated by a Hindu fanatic Nathuram Godse. With 'Hey Ram' on his lips, he breathed his last. The symbol of peace, truth and non-violence was gone forever. His memorial at Rajghat attracts people from around the world even today.

Sardar Vallabhbhai Patel

The Iron Man of India

(1875–1950)

Sardar Patel played a major role in the freedom struggle, but the work he carried out after India gained independence is more significant. The map of pre-independent India had two colours – yellow and pink. The pink colour represented those parts that were under British rule, while yellow depicted those 556 small princely states that were ruled by princes and kings. These states were given the choice by the British to join either the Indian Union or the newly formed state of Pakistan after partition. They also had the option of remaining independent states.

After independence in 1947, Sardar Patel was appointed the home minister and he took up the arduous task of bringing all these princely states under the Indian Union. He did so through talks, conciliation, appeasement, use of money and even force. Soon, all the princely states merged into the Indian Union. Only the Nizam of Hyderabad created a problem, but the use of police action made him comply with the wishes of Sardar Patel. This was how a strong India was formed. The work seemed impossible, but Sardar Patel displayed immense shrewdness and temperament and was successful in achieving his aim. It is because of this reason that he is called 'The Iron Man of India'.

Sardar Patel was born on 31 October 1875 at Nadiad in Gujarat, into a family of well-to-do landlords of the Leva Patidar caste. Being the fourth son of the family he always remained neglected, but he had strong will power. Sardar Patel married at the age of 16. He desired to go to England to study law, but his family was not able to bear the expenses. So after his matriculation at the age of 22, he cleared the district pleader's examination, which helped him practise law. In 1900 he established an independent

14

office of district pleader in Godhra and later moved to Borsad in Kheda district of Gujarat. His wife died in 1908 and he remained a widower. They had a son and a daughter.

In 1910 he went to London to study at Middleton. After clearing the examinations with flying colours, he returned to India in February 1913. He started his practice at the Ahmedabad bar and soon became a renowned barrister in criminal law. He was also known for his mannerisms and western style of dressing, was good at bridge and a member of the fashionable Gujarat Club.

It was in 1917 that he was first drawn towards Indian politics. It was during this time that Gandhiji entered politics. Gandhiji was particular that educated people of each region should be a part of his movement. In Bihar, he took Dr Rajendra Prasad and other lawyers into his fold. In Uttar Pradesh, he was closely associated with the Nehru family. In Gujarat, Gandhiji came across Sardar Patel. After their association with Gandhiji, all the leaders gave up their flourishing practice and joined the freedom struggle. The Sardar was deeply influenced by Gandhiji and his satyagraha movement. Though he did not support Gandhiji's policies wholly, he resolved to support Gandhiji. He gave up western clothes and dressed in white kurta and dhoti, clothes of the Indian farmer. He also quit the Gujarat Club.

He became the first Indian municipal commissioner of Ahmedabad in 1917. He held the post till 1924 and then became its elected municipal president from 1924 to 1928. In 1918 he planned mass rallies by organising the peasants, farmers and landowners of Kaira district to protest against the decision of the Bombay Government to collect the full annual revenue taxes in spite of crop failures caused by heavy rains. In 1928, he led the landowners of Bardoli in their protest against increased taxes. This was a successful campaign and it earned him the title of *sardar* (leader).

Like all political leaders he too had an independent point of view. In the early years of the freedom struggle, he believed in acquiring Dominion status for India rather than complete independence. Unlike Pt Nehru, Sardar Patel believed that armed revolution should be avoided because it would entail severe repression. And unlike Gandhiji, he did not believe that Hindu-Muslim unity was a prerequisite for independence. Sardar Patel had imbibed traditional values from his family so he did not believe in adopting a socialist pattern for India.

In the Lahore session of 1929, Sardar Patel was the second candidate after Gandhiji for the post of the presidency. Gandhiji opted out of the candidature because he did want the session to adopt the resolution for independence. He also forced Sardar Patel to withdraw because the latter opposed Hindu-Muslim unity. So Pt Nehru was elected the president of the session. In 1930, during the salt satyagraha, he was imprisoned for three months. Sardar Patel presided over the Karachi session of the Congress in 1931. He was arrested the following year in January only to be released in July 1934. After his release he campaigned vehemently for the Congress during the 1937 elections and was the main contender for the presidency of the 1937-38 session of the Congress. Again because of the intervention of Gandhiji, Sardar Patel withdrew and Pt Nehru became the president. Sardar Patel always acted with prudence and tact and accepted Gandhiji's wishes with diplomacy and always remained steadfast behind Pt Nehru. In October 1940 he was imprisoned along with other Congress leaders and released in August 1941. He was again imprisoned between August 1942 and June 1945.

When the Japanese attacked India during World War II, he rejected Gandhiji's non-violence. He opined that partition was in the interests of the country. Again because of the intervention of Gandhiji, in spite of being the leading candidate, Sardar Patel was not able to become the president of the Congress. Pt Nehru became the president of the Congress and he was invited by the British viceroy to form the interim government.

In 1947 India became independent. But the country was partitioned to satisfy the ideals of Jinnah and the Muslim League. Apart from Hyderabad and Junagadh, a few other princely states had Muslim rulers. Thanks to the efforts of Sardar Patel, they agreed to join the Indian Union. But the situation in Kashmir was different. Firstly, Kashmir shared its boundaries with Pakistan. Secondly, the people of Kashmir Valley were mostly Muslims, but the ruler was a Hindu. The ancestors of Pt Nehru were Kashmiris, so he looked after the affairs of Kashmir. Seeing the sensitive situation in Kashmir, Pakistan attacked Kashmir. It was then that Maharaja Hari Singh decided to accede to India. When he signed the pact, the army was sent to Srinagar to rescue the state from Pakistani tribals who had infiltrated into Kashmir. Before the tribals and the Pakistani army were evicted from Kashmir, a ceasefire was declared. So almost one-third of Kashmir was usurped by Pakistan.

Even after 1947–48, Pakistan attacked India twice and has indulged in clandestine warfare ever since. It trains young boys to disrupt the stability and unity of the country. The Kargil war makes it evident that Pakistan is trying to acquire Kashmir by hook or by crook. The only excuse they have to do so is that the majority of Kashmiris are Muslims. Some politicians believe that if Sardar Patel had been handed over the matter of Kashmir, the situation would have been in our favour today. When it came to decision-making, unlike Pt Nehru, Sardar Patel displayed sheer grit and determination. His one ambition in life was to have a united India.

After Independence, he worked for the welfare of the country with great enthusiasm. But the assassination of Gandhiji was a big blow for him. He had an undying love for Gandhiji. He considered Gandhiji as his elder brother and guru.

Between 1947 and 1950 he was the deputy prime minister, minister of home affairs, minister of information and minister of states.

On his death on 15 December 1950, the whole nation was plunged into grief. What Sardar Patel did in the 20th Century to unite the whole of India is unparalleled. Had it not been for Sardar Patel, India would still have been in fragments.

Bhagat Singh

The Great Revolutionary

(1907–1931)

India's freedom struggle was based on two schools of thought: the policy of non-violence advocated by Gandhiji and the extremist way – the seeds of which were sowed in the First War of Independence of 1857. Around the time the Congress launched the freedom struggle, a new generation of revolutionaries arose and their representative was Bhagat Singh.

Many Indians drew inspiration from the revolutionaries and were enthused by the idea of participating in the freedom struggle. And Bhagat Singh was the prime inspiration behind this feeling. The entire family of Bhagat Singh was involved in the freedom struggle. His father Kishan Singh was imprisoned for nationalist activities when Bhagat Singh was born. His uncle Sardar Ajit Singh had already been exiled for anti-British activities.

Bhagat Singh was born in September 1907 in Banga village (now in Pakistan) of Lyallpur district. His father was released for a few days from prison to see his newborn son. Bhagat Singh's early education was imparted in the village. Then he was sent to Lahore. In 1921 when the Non-cooperation Movement began, he was admitted to the National College where Punjab Kesari Lala Lajpat Rai, Bhai Parmanand and other patriotic leaders taught. On the insistence of Gandhiji, many students left government colleges. One of Bhagat Singh's classmates was Sukhdev, who was later a co-accused in the Bombay incident and was hanged along with him.

When Bhagat Singh was studying in college, his parents decided to get him married. Bhagat Singh ran off to Delhi, leaving behind a note saying that he was going off because he did not want to marry, and that they should not worry.

Bhagat Singh worked as a correspondent at *Dainik Arjun* in Delhi. Later, he went to Kanpur and worked for *Pratap*, a daily published by Ganesh Vidyarthi. It was here that he was introduced to Batukeshwar Dutt. During those days the rivers Ganga and Yamuna had caused great havoc in Kanpur. So these young men joined hands to serve the victims of the flood. It was here that Bhagat Singh met Chandra Shekhar Azad. Bhagat Singh was convinced that the country could gain independence only through revolution. So he established the *Naujavan Bharat Sabha* in 1924. Bhagat Singh, Sukhdev and Bhagwaticharan signed the declaration with their blood. To test the will power of the young members, Bhagat Singh placed his hand above the flame of a candle for 20 minutes. The flesh of his palm burnt and his compatriots had to forcefully remove his hand from the flame.

The people of India opposed the Simon Commission, so when it arrived in India, it was received with black flags. A band of peaceful protestors, which held a demonstration in Lahore, was clubbed mercilessly. Lala Lajpat Rai was gravely injured in the lathi-charge. He remained critical for a few days and then succumbed to his injuries. Bhagat Singh, Sukhdev and Rajguru killed the English officer Saunders who had hurt Lalaji.

In 1930, Bhagat Singh and Batukeshwar Dutt threw bombs in the Delhi Assembly, when the Public Safety Bill was being introduced. The Bill proposed to end the rights of workers to strike. Bhagat Singh and Dutt shouted slogans *Inquilaab zindabad* ("long live the revolution") and courted arrest. They were charged with many offences. Bhagat Singh, Sukhdev and Rajguru were found guilty in the Lahore bomb incident, the killing of Saunders, and the Assembly bombing case and sentenced to death.

In jail, Bhagat Singh and many of his associates went on a hunger strike demanding better conditions in prison. Bhagat Singh fasted for 115 days but Yatindra Das passed away on the 63rd day of the hunger strike. The large-scale agitation finally forced the government to concede their demands. On 23 March 1931 Bhagat Singh was hanged along with Sukhdev and Rajguru. The three patriots embraced death gallantly with the National Song on their lips.

Pt Jawaharlal Nehru

The First Prime Minister of India

(1889–1964)

India's first Prime Minister Pt Jawaharlal Nehru is considered the chief architect of modern India. He was the prime minister for 17 years, apart from the years he devoted towards India's freedom struggle. Pt Nehru's most significant contribution was to provide stability to parliamentary democracy. It is because of his efforts that our law-making body and the Press are independent, the bureaucracy does not interfere in politics and the role of the army is restricted to protecting the nation. Compare our state of affairs with that of Pakistan, which has faced a number of military coups and, after more than 50 years of existence, is still ruled by the army.

Jawaharlal Nehru was the son of Pt Motilal Nehru, a prominent lawyer of Allahabad and a leader of the independence struggle. Young Jawahar was educated at home by English tutors till the age of 16. In 1905, he was sent to Harrow. After two years at Harrow, he joined Trinity College, Cambridge for an Honours degree in Natural Science. By the time he left Cambridge, he had also earned a degree in law.

In March 1916, Pt Nehru married Kamala Kaul. Their only child, Indira Priyadarshini, was born on 19 November 1917. After his return from England he pursued law. But he found himself out of place in the company of lawyers. Like his peers, he wanted to take part in the freedom struggle.

Pt Nehru met Gandhiji for the first time in 1916 at the annual meeting of the Indian National Congress in Lucknow. Pt Nehru joined the Congress in 1919 just after the First World War. In 1921 many prominent freedom fighters were imprisoned. Pt Nehru went to jail for the first time then. During the freedom struggle he served nine periods of detention, which amounted to more than nine years in prison, the longest being the last, an imprisonment of three years that ended in June 1945. In 1923 he became the general secretary of the Congress for two years and again in 1927 for another two years. It was during those times that he was actually able to gauge the level of poverty and degradation of agriculture in India. This was to help him during his prime ministerial days ahead. In 1926-27, he toured Europe and Russia. He was deeply influenced by socialism and Marxism. During his imprisonment he was able to study Marxism in depth.

The Congress demanded Dominion status for India. In 1929, Pt Nehru was elected as the president of the historic Lahore Session that demanded *Purna Swaraj* (complete independence). This saw the emergence of Pt Nehru as the leader of the country's intellectuals and the youth. After his father's death in 1931, Pt Nehru became closer to Gandhiji. The Indians began to view him as the political heir of Gandhiji though Gandhiji himself did not officially designate him so until 1942. In March 1931 after the Gandhi-Irwin pact was signed, it was believed that peace would prevail between the Indians and the British. These hopes died when Lord Willingdon took over as the new viceroy. Gandhiji was arrested in January 1932 just after he returned from the Second Round Table Conference in London. Pt Nehru was imprisoned for two years.

India was given the right of self-governance under the Government of India Act 1935, which was the direct result of the Round Table Conferences. In early 1936 Kamala Nehru was taken to Europe to cure her illness but she died later in a sanitarium in Switzerland. Europe was reeling under the Second World War. Pt Nehru insisted that India would support England and France only as a free country.

The Congress Party came to power in a majority of states in the 1937 elections after the introduction of provincial autonomy under the Act of 1935. The Muslim League fared badly and their plea for the formation of coalition governments was rejected. This created differences between the Congress and the Muslim League, which later led to the partition of the country.

In September 1939, India was committed to the Second World War. The autonomous provincial ministries were not consulted, so the Congress withdrew its ministries as a mark of protest. Opinions differed on the subject. Gandhiji believed that the British should be supported unconditionally and any protest should be of a non-violent nature. Pt Nehru believed that in the war against Nazism, India should support the British only as a free nation.

In 1940, Pt Nehru was arrested and sentenced to four years' imprisonment. In 1942, when Japanese forces under the command of Netaji Subhash Chandra Bose reached the borders of India through Burma (now Myanmar), the British felt threatened. Sir Stafford Cripps, a member of the War Cabinet, was sent to India to initiate talks and bring about a settlement of the constitutional problem. The mission failed because Gandhiji wanted nothing short of independence. The Congress passed the Quit India resolution in Bombay (now Mumbai) on 8 August 1942. Gandhiji, Pt Nehru and the entire working committee of the Congress were arrested. Pt Nehru was released from his ninth and last detention only on 15 June 1945.

The Second World War came to an end in 1945. The Labour Party assumed power in Britain and sent a Cabinet Mission to India. Lord Mountbatten replaced Lord Wavell as the viceroy. No amicable solution could be reached, so the partition became inevitable. Much against the wishes of Gandhiji the country was partitioned into two independent countries – India and Pakistan. Pt Nehru became the first Prime Minister of India.

Gandhiji chose Pt Nehru as the president of the Congress at the 1929 Lahore Session. The attitudes of the two leaders were contrasting. Gandhiji had a religious bent of mind and wanted Indians to feel proud of India's past glories. Pt Nehru had a modern approach and a dream – to make India a self-reliant modern country. He wanted ancient thoughts, beliefs and traditions to co-exist with modern ones. This was because he had studied the history of developed countries and their political progress from close quarters during his Harrow days. So he was aware of the progress of science, technology and the economy.

Pt Nehru played a significant role in chalking out the direction of Indian politics and the Constitution. He wanted India to be a secular country. In spite of being a country with many castes, creeds, religions and languages, the people of the country are woven into the national fabric like yarns of different colours. Pt Nehru adopted modern values and ways of thinking and adapted them to suit Indian conditions. He wanted to carry India forward into the modern age of scientific and technical development. Pt Nehru felt the necessity of social concern for the poor and the underprivileged. And towards this effort the ancient Hindu Civil Code was reformed. This enabled Hindu widows to enjoy equality with men regarding matters of inheritance and property.

Pt Nehru's modern outlook attracted the younger intelligensia. He built a number of industries and dams for the progress of the country. He called them 'pilgrimage centres'. Pt Nehru developed public sector units so that capitalists of the country did not have a hold on the financial markets.

Partition brought with it a number of problems. Kashmir became a perennial problem. In 1948, Pakistan made an unsuccessful attempt to annex Kashmir. Pt Nehru was able to rid the country of Portuguese occupation of Goa. Another one of them was the Chinese aggression of 1962. Tibet was between China and India and it was given the status of a 'buffer state' by the British. The coining of the slogan 'Hindi-Chini Bhai-Bhai' and good neighbourly relations with the Chinese did not deter them from attacking India and occupying some parts in the north. Pt Nehru had blind faith in the Chinese but they had other intentions.

Pt Nehru's health showed signs of deterioration soon after the Chinese aggression. He suffered a mild stroke in 1963. In January 1964 he suffered another stroke. He died on 27 May the same year following a third and fatal stroke.

Some people believe that if Pt Nehru had not been in politics, he would have made a good historian or writer. Apart from his Autobiography, *The Glimpses of World History*, and *Letters to My Daughter from Prison* are significant works. Pt Nehru loved children very much. They called him "Chacha Nehru". Every year Children's Day is celebrated on 14 November, his birth anniversary.

Netaji Subhash Chandra Bose

The Fiery Revolutionary

(1897–1945)

Subhash Chandra Bose was a national leader who was faithfully associated for many years with the Congress party that followed Gandhiji's path of non-violence, but when he saw the atrocities of the British Government and the plight of the people, he chose a path totally different from Gandhiji's school of thought. He believed in the saying, 'An eye for an eye' and 'a tooth for a tooth'. And to rid the country of the British, he formed the Indian National Army (INA) or the Azad Hind Fauj.

The INA was an excellent example of social equality. The army consisted of people from different religions. But the spirit that united them all was their desire to release India from the bonds of slavery. The British Government was propagating the 'Divide and Rule' policy at that time. But Subhash Chandra Bose's efforts in forming the INA was a blow to the British policy and a symbol of national pride. And he set this example at a very young age.

When Bose was studying in school, the prevalent thought was that British children were superior to their Indian counterparts. The making of a revolutionary was witnessed when he beat an English boy in school to protest against this discrimination. When he was just 15, he told his mother that India was God's favourite country. He kept this thought kindled in his heart till the end of his life and also urged his followers to keep their solemn faith in India. He was of the opinion that no country in the world had the power to keep India in fetters for long. He had faith that India would soon gain independence.

Bose was born into a wealthy family in Cuttack. After completing his studies in India, he went to England to appear for the Indian Civil Services Examination. He cleared the examination and returned to India. But because of his patriotism, he gave up the ICS and joined the struggle for freedom.

Netaji Subhash Chandra Bose occupies a unique position in the history of India's struggle for independence. Though a member of the Congress, Bose took a different path in his struggle for Indian independence. The whole nation was excited when it learnt that Bose had gathered a large force to challenge the British and declare war to win India's independence.

The incident happened in 1940. There was a memorial named Dalhousie Square in Calcutta. The British claimed that in the First War of Independence in 1857, the Indians had burnt the hall after stuffing it with English men, women and children. The story, however, did not hold any water. This was an attempt to malign the Indians. Subhash Chandra Bose started a campaign to put an end to this memorial. Bose and his associates were imprisoned. Seeing the wrath of the Indians, the memorial was removed, but Bose was not released from prison.

In protest against the atrocities of the British, he went on a hunger strike on 20 November 1940. The British Government panicked and he was released from prison. But he was placed under house arrest amidst tight security. From then onwards Netaji's struggle for India's independence became famous.

The Second World War was on. But nobody could read Netaji's mind. During the house arrest, he grew a beard. This helped him disguise himself as a Pathan and flee from the clutches of the British to Peshawar. In Germany, Hitler was on his victory trail. Bose believed that it was best to befriend the enemy of one's enemy. So he met Hitler and sought his help. But it was difficult to fight for the cause of India from Germany. So after some time, he reached Japan in a submarine. He believed that Gandhiji's policy of non-violence could not help India in achieving freedom. So he founded the Indian National Army. He received the co-operation of Indians settled in Burma, Singapore etc. He called on patriots and said, "Give me your blood and I'll give you freedom." In February 1944, he had his first success. He was able to instil a sense of pride and devotion for India so that people were ready to make sacrifices for their homeland.

But the INA was not successful in liberating India. One of the major reasons was that in the predominantly marshy and thickly forested region, the weather led to the spread of malaria among the soldiers. Japan had to surrender to America after the latter used atom bombs. In Europe, Germany was defeated by the Allied Forces. The INA was successful in reaching Imphal. But because of the fall of Hitler, whom he considered his ally, Bose's dream of liberating India could not be successful. It is believed that he later died in an aircrash in Taiwan in 1945.

Jayprakash Narayan

The Lok Nayak

(1902–1979)

Jayprakash Narayan's life was different from the lives and times of ordinary leaders. When Indira Gandhi declared national Emergency, he was taken aback. He remained in hiding and organised a mass movement called the JP movement, aiming at total revolution. JP played a very significant role in the Quit India Movement. He led the movement heroically and successfully in Bihar, as a result of which the government lost all control over administration.

Jayprakash Narayan is among the few leaders who have received the respect and love of the masses. All through his life, he shied away from seeking a position in the government although he came across ample opportunities. Pt Jawaharlal Nehru offered him a place in his Cabinet, but he politely declined. After Pt Nehru's death, his name was proposed for the vacant position. Even when an opportunity to become the President of India arose, he put forward the name of Dr Zakir Hussain. He held the belief that once he had made up his mind to stay away from power, there was nothing that would lure him towards it.

Among many of his significant works was the solution that he found to solve the problem of the dacoits of Chambal. They created havoc in Chambal and the adjoining areas and were a constant headache to the government. Jayprakash Narayan was able to persuade them into surrendering before the government.

Jayprakash Narayan was born in Sitab Diyara village, about 50 km from Patna, the capital of Bihar, on 11 October 1902. He was the fourth child of Arsu Dayal and Phoolrani. His early education was completed at the village school. His nationalist feelings were strong even when he was a teenager and he took to wearing khadi. He completed his intermediate from Bihar Vidyapeeth.

At this moment in life, he was not sure about his future plans when he was married to Prabhavati, the daughter of a prominent leader Brijkishore. He was then 18 years old and she was only 14. As she was very young, she was not sent to her husband's place, instead she was sent to Sabarmati Ashram to stay with Gandhiji and Kasturba Gandhi. Then he enrolled at California University in America. In the seven years that he spent abroad, he was deeply influenced by Marxist philosophy.

When he returned to India in 1929, he was faced with a strange dilemma. He met his wife at Gandhiji's ashram. She was influenced deeply by the thought of celibacy during her stay at the ashram. Jayprakash respected her sentiments, and in spite of being husband and wife, both practised celibacy.

On the political front, he joined the Congress in 1929. When he came over to Allahabad from Bihar, he came in contact with Pt Nehru. In 1932, he was imprisoned in Nasik Jail for one year for his participation in the Civil Disobedience Movement. There he came in contact with Ram Manohar Lohia, Minoo Masani, Achyut Patwardhan, Ashok Mehta, Yusuf Meherali, Morarji Desai and other national leaders. When he was released, he formed the Congress Socialist Party, a left-wing group within the Congress.

In 1939, he was again imprisoned for protesting against Indian participation in the Second World War, but he escaped. He tried to rally the masses against British rule but along with his revolutionaries he was arrested in 1943. He wanted the Congress to adopt a militant policy against the British.

After India gained independence, JP formed the All India Congress Socialist Party along with Acharya Narendra Dev. In 1953, he helped in the merger of the Krishak Mazdoor Praja parties. In 1972, he came in contact with Vinoba Bhave and joined Vinoba's *Bhoodan* Movement. It was during this time that his wife died of cancer. Though it was a big loss for him, he continued to serve the people.

He shot into prominence in 1974, when he openly criticised the Congress Government for misrule and large-scale corruption. In 1975, when the Allahabad High Court convicted Indira Gandhi for resorting to corrupt electoral practices, JP called for her resignation. However, Indira Gandhi declared a national Emergency. JP and other prominent leaders were arrested. When he was released after five months, his movement against corruption, called the JP movement, gathered momentum. He was able to unite different political parties like the Jan Sangh, the Socialists, the Congress (O) and the Bharatiya Lok Dal under a new banner – the Janata Party. In the 1977 elections, the Janata Party was able to rout the Congress to form the first non-Congress government after Independence. Though his was the most important contribution, he stayed away from power and let Morarji Desai take over the reigns of the government.

Soon his health deteriorated and he had to be kept on dialysis. On 8 October 1979 he died. He was honoured with the Bharat Ratna posthumously in 1999.

Lokmanya Tilak

The Spirit of Swaraj

(1856–1920)

It is necessary to include Lokmanya Bal Gangadhar Tilak in the list of famous Indians of the 20th Century because it was largely due to his efforts that the feeling of pride and self-respect was aroused among Indians. He never believed in the policy of pleading for one's rights. He was the one who formed the extremist wing of the Congress because he believed in acquiring rights by force. And the thought had many takers. Among his supporters were Bipin Chandra Pal and Lala Lajpat Rai. And the triad – Lal, Bal, Pal – supported the extremist wing of the Congress. It was Tilak who coined the slogan "Swaraj is my birthright."

Bal Gangadhar Tilak was born on 23 July 1856 in Ratnagiri district of Maharashtra. His father, Gangadhar Rao, was a scholar in Sanskrit and grammar. He was fearless and had great self-respect – the qualities inherited by his son. Even during his school years, he was respected by his companions. He was moved by the plight of the poor and was always ready to serve them. The people considered him worthy of respect and addressed him as 'Tilak'.

Tilak tried to revive a sense of pride among Hindus for their ancient culture and traditions. Tilak's statement "Swaraj is my birthright and I shall have it" was considered anti-government. Fearless that he was, he worked undaunted for the independence of India.

Lokmanya Tilak married at the young age of 15, but after graduating, he joined the freedom struggle. For the dissemination of nationalist thoughts, he first opened a school, then he began publishing two newspapers – *Mahratta* in English and *Kesari* in

Marathi. To invoke a sense of national pride, he wrote provocative articles against the British Government. So he had to face several punishments and imprisonments. To instil a sense of unity, he organised 'Ganesh Chaturthi' and 'Shivaji Jayanti'. He celebrated and popularised these occasions as great festivals.

He spent six months' rigorous imprisonment in Mandalay Jail, Burma due to his alleged support for the murder of a British couple. The more the punishment imposed on him, the more his fame grew and the more people revered him. The British tried to stop the publication of his newspapers.

Lokmanya Tilak was a scholar of Sanskrit, Mathematics, Astrology, History and Philosophy. He was also a great writer. Among the significant books he wrote, were *The Secret of the Gita, Orion, The True Home of the Aryans* and others. *The Secret of the Gita* is an annotation of the Holy *Gita* which believes that work is worship.

Lokmanya Tilak was the symbol of Indianness. The youth respected him. The public had profound reverence for him. On his death, Gandhiji remarked, "The public considers Lokmanya Tilak as a god and his words as words from the *Vedas*."

In 1920, he was chosen the president of the Congress, but he died in July before the session. Lokmanya Tilak was one of the greatest nationalist leaders whom his countrymen can never forget.

Madan Mohan Malaviya

The Epitome of Indian Culture

(1861–1946)

A mong the prominent personalities of the 20th Century, there was one person who could be called India's foremost monk. And the speciality of this monk was that he got donations in lakhs, but never spent a penny of the donations on himself.

Malaviyaji had pledged that the modern education system be modified and developed to suit the Indian context. And so he established the Benares Hindu University. He collected donations from kings, princes, financers and industrialists for the purpose. Malaviyaji commanded a lot of respect and so, nobody could give him less than a few lakhs. Malaviyaji's efforts to save Hindu culture, thereby contributing to the rejuvenation of Indian culture, made him one of the prominent Indians of the 20th Century.

Malaviyaji also tried to foil the growing influence and coercion of Christianity and Islam. Just as Ashutosh Mukherjee strived for the propagation of education and science in Bengal, Malaviyaji tried to safeguard Indian culture by establishing the Hindu University. The University had the pride of having Dr S. Radhakrishnan as one of its Vice-Chancellors.

Malaviyaji was an Indian to the core through his mind, body and dress code. He was always dressed in homespun cloth. He wore a long white *angrakha*, a *tilak* on his forehead and a white Khaddar or homespun cloth as a turban. All his life he tried to safeguard Indian culture from the influence of the West.

He was born on 25 December 1861 at Allahabad in a *Karamkandi* Brahmin family. His father Brijnath Malaviya was a Sanskrit scholar and devoted most of his time to virtuous predisposition. After completing his education, Malaviyaji was compelled to take up teaching as a profession, though his desire was to take up politics. Even while in school, he was fond of writing poems and plays. He wrote under the pseudonym 'Makrand'. He considered poet Bharatendu as his guru. He devoted his whole life to teaching and his greatest achievement was the Benares Hindu University. The University has a memorial in recognition of his contribution.

Malaviyaji also excelled as a journalist. Apart from *Hindustan*, the King of Kalankar, Rampal Singh brought out *Leader* and *The Hindustan Times* with the help of Malaviyaji. Then Malaviyaji left the editorial work of *Hindustan* and studied law. He went on to become one of the distinguished lawyers of Allahabad. He gave up his practice in 1911, but took up the case of the accused in the infamous Chauri Chaura incident of 1922 and got them acquitted before the Allahabad High Court. He was chosen the president of the Congress at the Lahore Congress Session held in 1909. He went to jail several times in connection with the freedom struggle. He died on 12 November 1946.

In spite of being an eminent scholar and a prominent leader, he never gave up the Indian way of dressing and culture. He was the epitome of Indian culture.

Maulana Abul Kalam Azad

Theologian and Prominent Leader

(1888–1958)

Maulana Azad was born in Mecca, Saudi Arabia, to an eminent Indian scholar and an Arab mother. He was brought up and educated strictly along Islamic lines in Calcutta, but he secretly learned English. However, in spite of his firm belief in Islam, he did not accept the partition of India on religious grounds. Maulana Azad worked towards the solidarity of the nation and was never influenced by religious fundamentalism.

Not many people are aware of the contribution he made towards the freedom struggle. Maulana Azad never came to the limelight and let Gandhiji and Pt Nehru take all the credit. He even formed the Nationalist Muslim Party within the Congress to disprove the claim of the Muslim League that it represented all Muslims. Pt Jawaharlal Nehru considered Azad a symbol of courage and culture.

Maulana Azad founded the University Grants Commission. His contribution towards psychological study and technical education is also immense. He also founded the All India Council for Technical Education.

On the one hand, he showed an interest in adult literacy, female literacy, scientific and technical education and higher education; on the other, he also worked for the acknowledgement of arts, music and literature at the national level. He founded the Sahitya Akademi, the Sangeet Natak Akademi and the Lalit Kala Akademi with much zeal. Sahitya Akademi is a national organisation and promotes literature in all the prominent languages of India by giving awards to the best writers in regional languages. When the Sahitya Akademi was founded, it did not have a building. Maulana Azad gave a portion of his house to set up an office of the Akademi. In his 10-year stint as education minister, Maulana Azad contributed a lot for the promotion of education, art and literature.

Maulana Azad was a recipient of many literary awards. He also translated the Koran. Maulana Azad had a firm belief in Islam. His life is an example of the impact religion makes on a true follower. Pt Nehru said that Azad was an ideal religious person.

He said the following words to the people affected by the communal riots immediately after Partition.

Chalo Aao Tumhe Dikhayein
Jo Bacha Hai Mahatal-e-Shehar Mein
Ahal-e-Sidak Ki Turbatein

(Come, I'll show you what is left of the town of executioners. Here lie the graves of true, honest and religious men.)

Maulana Azad was known for his integrity. In his book, *India Wins Freedom*, he blames both the Congress leaders and Mohammad Ali Jinnah for the partition of the country. He was strongly opposed to partition.

He passed away on 22 February 1958. He was posthumously awarded India's highest civilian award, the Bharat Ratna in 1992.

Veer Savarkar

Revolutionary Hindu Activist

(1883–1966)

Vinayak Damodar Savarkar is better remembered as Veer Savarkar because he faced the atrocities of the British Raj with great fortitude. When he was exiled to the Andamans, he was yoked to the milling machine and made to extract 30 pounds of mustard oil by crushing. The young lad was very brave, but the atrocities damaged his health and he could never lead a healthy life. And when the *Hindi-Chini Bhai-Bhai* chanting Chinese attacked India, he was shocked. On 26 February 1966, he fell unconscious and died subsequently.

Veer Savarkar was born on 28 May 1883 at Nasik in Maharashtra. He was fondly called Tatya. He had two brothers. Their parents narrated them stories from the *Ramayana* and the *Mahabharata* and also the adventurous tales of Shivaji and Maharana Pratap. So the feeling of patriotism was instilled in Savarkar right from childhood. Maharashtra had produced another valiant hero, Lokmanya Tilak. When Veer Savarkar met Tilak, his spirit of nationalism became stronger.

The effect of the influence was that whenever a couple or more boys met, they discussed patriotism. Even in his school, he constituted a group called 'Mitramandali'. Gradually his influence increased and people praised him.

After completing his BA, he wanted to study law. So he went to London. But he met a few Indian revolutionaries there who made plans against the British Empire and gave them shape. The chief revolutionaries were Shyamji Krishna Verma and Madanlal Dhingra. Savarkar stayed at India House in London, which had by then become the centre of Indian revolutionary activities. Savarkar, who was already a patriot, now began to participate in the activities of the revolutionaries with more vigour. So the British Government sent him back to India. But he jumped off the ship that was carrying him back to India because he wanted to be a free man. However, the officials caught him and transported him to the Andamans. His brother Ganesh Savarkar was also undergoing imprisonment in the same jail. Savarkar stayed there for 10 years. After he was released, he was kept under house arrest in Ratnagiri. It was here that he met Subhash Chandra Bose.

Behind the thin, frail body was the strong, resonating mind of a Hindu activist. He also wanted to develop the feeling of Hindu activism as a strong force. And towards this end, he founded the Hindu Mahasabha. He invoked the feeling of self-pride among Hindus. In 1948, he was arrested for alleged involvement in the assassination of Mahatma Gandhi, but the court did not find him guilty of any conspiracy. Savarkar did not have any malice towards anyone. His acts of patriotism and the sufferings he faced on the path of national struggle are proof enough that he was totally committed to the cause of nationalism.

He considered the Hindu Mahasabha as the Hindu National Mahasabha. The Hindu Mahasabha participated in a number of elections, but in a country that was influenced by the views of Mahatma Gandhi, it failed to achieve success.

Veer Savarkar was also a good writer. His work *The First War of National Independence* is considered very significant.

Aruna Asaf Ali

An Icon of Courage

(1909–1996)

The courageous and defiant Aruna Asaf Ali finds a place of honour in India's independence struggle and socialist revolution. Initially she was associated with the Congress and in 1948, after Independence, she joined the Socialist Party of Acharya Narendra Dev. Later she joined the Communist Party and remained associated with the party till the end through the presidentship of their *Patriot* group of newspapers.

Aruna Asaf Ali gained instant fame and recognition for the valour she displayed in 1942 during the Quit India Movement when she broke the police barricade and hoisted the Congress flag at Oval Maidan in Bombay. This was a task well achieved for a 30-year-old lady. She went into hiding after the incident and resurfaced in 1946, after the new government formed by the Congress withdrew the arrest warrant issued against her. The secret service of the British Government had announced a reward of Rs 5,000 – a big amount in those days – for anyone who could provide clues about her whereabouts. Her property and wealth were impounded too. Yet she could not be caught. Although she went into hiding, she did not remain inactive. She toured the country and instilled a feeling of nationalism among the masses.

Aruna was born into a Bengali family on 16 July 1909 in Kalka (Haryana). Her father was a doctor, but he died when she was too young. Her mother sent her to Nainital for studies, where she came in contact with the Nehru family. This association instilled political awareness in her. After returning from Nainital, she joined a school in Calcutta. On one occasion, when she went to Allahabad to meet her sister, she met a well-known Muslim lawyer Asaf Ali. The meeting soon blossomed into love and they got married. Both participated in the activities of the Congress together. In 1930, she was imprisoned at Lahore for a year for her participation in the satyagraha movement. Again in 1932, she was jailed for six months. These sentences made her stronger from within and helped her carry out the courageous feat of 1942.

After Independence, she settled in Delhi and dedicated herself to social service. She was also elected the Mayor of Delhi in 1958. She published a magazine, *Link* and established 'Saraswati Bhavan' – an institution that was concerned with education and service to the poor and underprivileged.

In 1992, she was awarded the Jawaharlal Nehru Award for International Understanding. In recognition of her services, the government conferred the Bharat Ratna on her posthumously in 1997.

Aruna Asaf Ali left for her heavenly abode on 29 July 1996.

Lala Lajpat Rai

Punjab Kesari

(1865–1928)

In the 20th Century, there have been many fearless national leaders who never hesitated in taking up challenges. Netaji Subhash Chandra Bose is an illustrious example of such a leader. And there was another – Punjab Kesari Lala Lajpat Rai. He was loved and respected not only in India, but also in America. His life is a tale of supreme sacrifice. In spite of coming from a well-to-do family, he chose to serve the nation. He protested against the Simon Commission before Bredma Hall in Lahore and took the brunt of the lathi charge over his head. And this led to his untimely demise.

He hailed from Punjab and always spoke in chaste Punjabi. His khaddar turban was his identity. He toured the world, but never gave up his identity and his pride of being an Indian.

His fearlessness and sense of social service earned him the title of Punjab Kesari. Lala Lajpat Rai was born on 28 January 1865 into an Agarwal family in a small village named Jagraon in Moga district of Punjab. After his formal education, he went to Lahore to study. He practised at Lahore and Hisar. At Lahore, he helped establish the nationalist Anglo-Vedic School and became a follower of Swami Dayanand, the founder of the Arya Samaj. Slowly his area of work expanded. He travelled across the nation and helped people suffering from famine.

At 23, he joined the Congress. It was because of his zealous efforts that the Congress Session at Lahore in 1893 became a success. The British Government saw the makings of a revolutionary in Lalaji and exiled him to Mandalay Jail in Burma (now Myanmar) in May 1907 without any trial. However because of lack of sufficient evidence, he was allowed to return in November the same year.

In December 1907 the supporters of Lalaji wanted to elect him the president of the Congress, but leaders who believed in seeking favours from the British refused to accept him. Because of differences, the party split.

Lala Lajpat Rai realised that there was a lack of nationalism among the youth of Punjab. So he established the Lok Sevak Sangh to provide financial assistance to those youths who were engaged in the service of the nation. During the Second World War, he went to the United States. He returned in 1919. In 1920, he led the special session of the Congress that launched the Non-cooperation Movement. Between 1921 and 1923, he was put in prison. On his release he was elected to the Legislative Assembly.

In 1928, he introduced the Legislative Assembly resolution for the boycott of the Simon Commission. When the Simon Commission came to India, it was boycotted by the whole nation. In Lahore, Lalaji led a protest march against the Commission. The peace marchers were mercilessly lathi-charged. Lalaji received a blow on his head and was badly injured. A few days later, on 17 November 1928 he succumbed to his injuries. Later, revolutionaries killed Superintendent Saunders, the police officer who was responsible for Lalaji's death.

In the Congress, the triad of Lal (Lala Lajpat Rai), Bal (Bal Gangadhar Tilak) and Pal (Bipin Chandra Pal) were very famous.

Lala Lajpat Rai wrote a number of books. Some of the prominent ones include *The Story of My Deportation* (1908), *Arya Samaj* (1915), *The United States of America: A Hindu's Impression* (1916) and *Unhappy India* (1928).

C. Rajagopalachari

First Governor-General of India

(1878–1972)

Chakravarti Rajagopalachari, better known as Rajaji, was a freedom fighter, statesman, scholar, thinker, humorist and humanist. Along with Gandhi, Nehru and Patel, he was one of the strong pillars of the Indian National Congress. After Independence he succeeded Lord Mountbatten as the Governor-General of India.

Born on 10 December 1878 at Thorapalli village in Hosur taluka of Salem district to Chakravarti Iyengar and Singaramma, C. Rajagopalachari graduated from the Presidency College, Madras. He received his Bachelor of Law degree in 1899. After this, he started practice in Salem in 1900, and soon reached the peak of glory in his profession. He won practically all his cases. Rajaji had met Gandhiji in 1919 and like the latter he was upset by the Rowlatt Committee recommendations. Later he became Gandhiji's lieutenant in the south. During the freedom struggle, Rajaji was jailed several times.

Rajaji also organised a successful Flag Satyagraha in Nagpur in 1923. Like Gandhiji he too transgressed the Salt Act on 13 April 1930, by leading a 150-mile march of 98 satyagrahis from Trichy to Vedarnyam. Rajaji played a leading part in shaping the Poona Pact. He had the unique ability of resolving differences between Hindus and Muslims and for that reason he was made the Governor of Bengal in 1947.

Later when the term of Lord Mountbatten ended, Rajaji was made the first Governor-General of India. He was awarded the Bharat Ratna in 1954.

Rajaji passed away on 25 December 1972.

Lal Bahadur Shastri

Leader of Towering Integrity

(1904–1966)

Although Lal Bahadur Shastri was just five feet in height and had a thin physique, he was a leader of towering integrity. Shastriji became the Prime Minister of India after the death of Pt Nehru. This surprised many, as Shastriji came from a humble background. But he rose to the position of prime minister solely on merit and it was because of these qualities that Pt Nehru had faith in his competence.

His competence was proved immediately after he took over as prime minister. At that time Pakistan was ruled by the dictator Marshal Ayub Khan. Pt Nehru's death was hastened because, in 1962, China invaded India in spite of our cordial relations. Panchsheel and *Hindi-Chini Bhai-Bhai* failed miserably. This was a shock for Pt Nehru and he could not recover from it. After Shastriji took over as the prime minister, he showed tremendous courage and was not deterred by the threats of Ayub Khan. Shastriji said that if Pakistan had its eyes on Delhi, we will protect it, and will gallantly reach Lahore. Shastriji won great popularity for the firmness with which he handled the issue of Kashmir.

In the war that ensued, the Indian Army took large parts of Pakistan. The army laid siege to Lahore, which was within firing range of army tanks. It was at this juncture that the now defunct Soviet Union intervened. Both the leaders went to Tashkent for negotiations. On the advice of the USSR, India agreed to hand over all the captured areas back to Pakistan. After he signed the Tashkent Agreement with President Ayub Khan, Indian forces withdrew from Pakistan. Perhaps Shastriji thought that people back home would not like his decision. He went to sleep with a heavy heart. He suffered a heart attack at night and died in his sleep.

Shastriji was born into a Kayastha family on 2 October 1904 in the town of Mughalsarai, Uttar Pradesh. In the initial stages of his life, he suffered many hardships. His father, Sharda Prasad Srivastava, was a teacher. Shastriji's father died when he was just an infant. So his mother Ramdulari Devi took him to her father's home. As he had a small frame even as a child, he was called *Nanhe*.

Some accounts state that Shastriji used to swim across the Ganges to reach school because he did not have the money to pay the boatman who ferried people across the river. After completing his fifth standard, he was sent to his uncle Raghunath's house in Varanasi where he was admitted to Harishchandra High School. Because of his pleasing manners and interest in studies, he soon became a favourite among his teachers. It was during these days that Bal Gangadhar Tilak, the nationalist leader, paid a visit to Varanasi. His words left an indelible impact on young Shastriji's mind. Inspired by Tilak and the Non-cooperation Movement, he left school although he was required to sit through just another month to complete high school.

On one occasion, he participated in a protest rally during the Non-cooperation Movement. Though he was around 16 at that time, he seemed a young boy of around 12–13 because of his short stature and frail frame. The police arrested him along with the other protestors, but let him go after questioning because they mistook him to be a boy.

It was during those days that Madan Mohan Malaviya established the Kashi Vidyapeeth (now Mahatma Gandhi Kashi Vidyapeeth). Shastriji sought admission in the institute and obtained the title of *Shastri* (learned in the Scriptures).

After completing his education, he sought a source of livelihood. Lala Lajpat Rai had just established the Lok Seva Mandal. Inspired by Lalaji's ideals, Shastriji became a life member of the institution and dedicated himself to the service of the people. The institution provided its members a monthly stipend but that could barely fulfil the basic needs of a family. Shastriji was married to Lalita Devi when he was just 17. It was because of his wife's whole-hearted cooperation that it became easier for Shastriji to work for the freedom struggle. It is said that Shastriji accepted just a spinning wheel and handspun khadi cloth as dowry.

As part of his work at the Lok Sevak Mandal, he used to visit Allahabad and there he came in contact with Pt Nehru. He was appointed the general secretary of the Allahabad Congress Committee. Between 1930 and 1945, he participated in a number of movements and spent almost nine years in prison.

In 1942, when Gandhiji gave the call for 'Quit India', he was arrested along with other prominent leaders in Bombay. He, however, escaped and reached Allahabad. He held the belief that before embarking on a new venture, one should take the blessings of one's mother. He reached home at four o'clock in the morning and took his mother's blessings. Exactly at five, he went to Allahabad Square and addressed thousands of people gathered there. Here the police arrested him.

In 1937 and 1946, Shastriji was elected to the Legislature of the United Provinces. After Independence, he served as Minister of Home Affairs and Transportation in the Uttar Pradesh Government. In 1952, Shastriji was elected to the Central Legislature. Pt Nehru later appointed him as the Railway Minister in the Central Cabinet. But in August 1956, when a terrible rail mishap occurred near Mehboob Nagar, he resigned owning moral responsibility. Such instances of humility made him a highly respected personality.

In 1961, he was appointed the Minister for Home Affairs. In early 1964, when Pt Nehru took ill, he was appointed Minister without Portfolio and later, in June 1964, he became the prime minister after Pt Nehru's death.

Shastriji was posthumously honoured with the Bharat Ratna in 1966.

Dadabhai Naoroji

Founder-Member of the INC

(1825–1917)

Dadabhai Naoroji is one of those personalities who were respected by the British and also honoured by Indians. He was considered to be a father-figure among nationalists, being a founder-member of the Indian National Congress (INC). Dadabhai not only worked towards attaining independence but also inspired many educated people to join hands with him.

Dadabhai Naoroji was born on 4 September 1825 in a Parsi family. In 1845, he did his B.A. and ten years later went to London. There, he assisted Bhikhaji Cama, a leading businessman, in his business. He organised the Indians living in London and formed the Indian Society. After some time he was chosen to be a member of the British Parliament. One of the first Indians to have the honour of becoming a member of the British Parliament, he was known as "The Grand Old Man of India".

When Dadabhai joined the Congress, it was basically a society of government servants and its main function was to apprise the British Government about the people's problems. Dadabhai was extremely popular and was elected as its president in 1896 and 1906. Dadabhai was not satisfied with merely forwarding complaints to the government. He sought independence. He was summoned to court for his activities.

Dadabhai Naoroji is among those leaders who did not overlook the importance of keeping in touch with the British while demanding independence. He is also acclaimed as the "Father of Indian Politics and Economics".

Dadabhai Naoroji passed away on 30 June 1917 at Versova at the age of 91.

Gopal Krishna Gokhale

The Gem of Maharashtra

(1866–1915)

He has been aptly called by Lokmanya Tilak, his lifelong rival, "The diamond of India, the gem of Maharashtra." Gokhale was born on 9 May 1866 at Kotluk in Ratnagiri district in the Kolhapur State of Bombay Presidency. He came from a poor Brahmin family. In 1884, he graduated from Elphinstone College, Bombay. Gokhale's brother wanted him to go to England and compete for the ICS, but he chose the humbler profession of teaching. Later he came under the influence of Justice Ranade, and under his expert guidance studied Indian Economics.

In 1900, he was elected a member of the Bombay Legislative Council, where he worked along with Sir Pherozeshah Mehta. In 1902, he was nominated to the Viceroy's Council, where his budget speeches were well known for financial criticism.

He was elected the president of the National Congress at Benares in 1905. His presidential speech is considered one of the best ever delivered on the Congress platform. Gokhale was a champion of the interests of Indians abroad. He supported their agitation in South Africa against the humiliating restraints imposed upon them. This interest in the South African problem brought him into close contact with Gandhi. He supported Gandhi's passive resistance campaign.

He played a significant role in India's freedom movement. For years he stood forth, in the eyes of both the Indian Government and the British, as the most representative Indian. He never merely criticised the government when he dealt with its shortcomings, as some of his contemporaries did. He was, in a larger sense, a reconciler between Western and Eastern culture. Gandhi affirmed Gokhale as his political guru. He died on 19 February 1915.

Chandra Shekhar Azad

The Undaunted Revolutionary

(1905-1931)

Chandra Shekhar Azad will always remain immortal in the annals of history as a man who sacrificed his life at the altar of freedom. At a time when Gandhiji was busy with his *ahimsa* and Non-cooperation Movement to liberate the country, a couple of fiery young men were sceptical about his methods. They were sure the best course was the proverbial policy of 'tit for tat' and were in favour of giving the British a fitting reply for their tyranny. Bhagat Singh, Sukhdev, Sachindra Sanyal and Ram Prasad Bismil were among those who had no faith in non-violence. While Bhagat Singh was active in Punjab, Chandra Shekhar Azad was busy in UP. He was fired by the zeal to help Bhagat Singh and when the two collaborated, Chandra Shekhar Azad was given the leadership of the activists.

Azad became a member of the group which had vowed to avenge the death of Lala Lajpat Rai. British police officer Saunders was their target. The group looted the government treasury for funds required for the movement. A terror to the police, Azad was listed a terrorist and kept under watch. He was surrounded on 27 February 1931 in Alfred Park, Allahabad, by a strong police squadron Azad fought them bravely for many hours. Even after he was killed, the British dared not approach his body and waited for some time to confirm his death.

Azad was born on 23 July 1906 at Jhabra in Madhya Pradesh. He ran away from home when young, reached Kashi (Benares) and joined the freedom struggle. In 1921, he was first sentenced to 15 lashes for revolutionary activities. With each stroke of the whip the young patriot shouted *Bharat Mata ki Jai and confounded the officers with his undaunted spirit.*

Political Leaders

Indira Gandhi

India's First Woman Prime Minister

(1917–1984)

Indira Gandhi is one of those leaders who is known more for the wrong reasons. But the sheer grit and determination she displayed by siding with the Shanti Vahini Army and helping in the formation of Bangladesh is laudable.

Indira Priyadarshini Gandhi, the only child of Jawaharlal and Kamala Nehru, was born on 19 November 1917 in Allahabad. Pt Nehru was the first Prime Minister of India. But the beliefs and works of father and daughter make it clear that the thoughts and inclinations of both were totally different. The Congress was divided when she was the president of the party and she was often accused of manipulation to keep power in her own hands, but such was not the case with Pt Nehru. There is no denying the fact that Indira was a true patriot like her father, but never in her childhood or her youth did she ever give an indication that she would transform into such a steadfast personality.

There were many ups and downs during her prime ministerial days. She remained the Prime Minister of India for almost 17 years. And to govern a vast country like India which had varied cultures, languages and customs, was definitely a challenge and Indira faced it with immense courage. And by doing so, she changed the image of India in the South Asian scenario.

After the partition of the country in 1947, Pakistan was divided into two – East and West. And having a Pakistan-administered state on either side of India was creating a problem. In the 1971 war with Pakistan, she helped East Pakistan severe ties with West Pakistan and created an independent state of Bangladesh. In doing so, she displayed tremendous determination and diplomacy.

But she also received a lot of flak for her other activities, especially for declaring Emergency in the country in 1975, at a time when the situation was not at all grim. The reason for declaring an Emergency was that the Congress was losing hold of power in the country and Indira Gandhi wanted to make sure that her position as the prime minister remained unchallenged. A number of important leaders and journalists were arrested. Freedom of the Press was curbed.

When she was young, most people called her a 'dumb doll'. It would have been nobody's guess that this 'dumb doll' would go on to become a powerful figure.

Indira's life can be broadly divided into three phases. First – her childhood, where she was forced to play with toys, dolls, and tin soldiers because her mother Kamala Nehru always remained ill and her father Pt Nehru mostly spent his life in jail. Inspired by the freedom struggle and seeing freedom fighters at close quarters when they came to discuss political strategies with her father and grandfather Motilal Nehru, she formed the 'monkey brigade'.

The second phase of her life began when she was in England. Her mother was then taken to Switzerland for treatment. It was here that she met Feroze Gandhi. It is believed that driven by emotions, she married him in haste and repented later. For most of their married life, they lived separately. After Partition and Independence, when Pt Nehru became the prime minister, she lived with her father to look after him. Kamala Nehru had died and there was no one to look after her father. Feroze and Indira had two sons, but her marital life was not happy.

The third phase of her life began in 1955 when she became an active member of the Indian National Congress. In 1959 she was elected to the post of party president, which was largely an honorary post. After Pt Nehru died, Lal Bahadur Shastri became the Prime Minister of India and included her in the Cabinet as Information & Broadcasting Minister. In 1966 she became the Prime Minister after Shastriji's sudden demise. This period was completely different from the other two phases of her life. It was during this period that she proved Shakespeare's statement, "Frailty, thy name is woman", wrong.

She took a few steps that prove that besides being fearless, she was a great patriot. She nationalised all banks. She also discontinued the privy purses that were being paid to all those kings who had agreed to join the Indian Union after Independence in exchange for the privy purses. In doing so, she ended their hold on their ancestral land and property.

But her leadership was under constant challenge from Morarji Desai. In the elections of 1967, the Congress won by a slender margin, so she had to accept Desai as the deputy prime minister. But in the elections of 1971, she was able to win by a huge margin. She supported the cause of East Bengal (now Bangladesh) in its secessionist conflict with Pakistan in 1971. The Indian Army was able to win a decisive victory over Pakistan and helped in the creation of Bangladesh. This was carried out in spite of America's protest. This act of hers was a challenge to those western forces who believed that South Asia was a region where they could carry out their selfish motives.

In the national elections held in March 1972, the Congress registered a landslide victory. But her opponents accused her of violating electoral laws and in June 1975, the High Court of Allahabad ruled against her. She was to be deprived of her seat in Parliament and debarred from active politics for six years. It was then that she declared Emergency in the country. She assumed emergency powers and most of her political opponents were imprisoned. There were curbs on personal freedom. Many harsh policies were implemented, which made the party unpopular during the time.

When the long postponed elections were finally held in 1977, the Congress party was routed. The Janata Party took over after Indira Gandhi left office following the defeat of her party.

In 1931, she attended the Congress Session for the first time with her father. In 1938, she became a member of the Congress and participated in the freedom struggle. In 1947, when Pt Nehru became the prime minister, she accompanied him on tours across the nation and helped him in carrying out his duties.

To curb the growing violence in Punjab, she carried out Operation Bluestar, which was an example of great fortitude. But as a result, Punjab was plunged into terrorist violence for almost 10 years.

After her defeat in '77, she campaigned with much fanfare. The Janata Party came to power in '77, but did not deliver as per the expectations of the electorate. So the people voted her back to power in the 1980 elections. In October 1984, she was assassinated by her own Sikh security guards in retaliation for Operation Bluestar.

Taking a retrospective of Indira's life, it is clear that she was never afraid of difficulties. She faced every problem with courage and fortitude.

Shyama Prasad Mukherjee

Founder of Jan Sangh

(1901–1953)

The 20th Century brought a number of opportunities for India, but also a tragedy. And that was the partition of the country on a communal basis, mainly due to the British Government's inclination towards the Muslim community. Gandhiji was not in favour of partition and was willing to give all possible help to the Muslims. As matters worsened, Muslims got all the sympathy and Hindus began to be called communal. During the early days, Jammu & Kashmir was ruled by Sheikh Abdullah. He had the same powers as the Prime Minister of India and the state even had its own flag. The leader of the Citizen's Council Pt Premnath Dogra and other Hindus wanted to hoist the national flag. However, their requests were turned down by Sheikh Abdullah at the instance of Pt Nehru. When Dr Shyama Prasad Mukherjee went to Jammu to resolve the issue, he was arrested. He died in a jail in Kashmir.

When Hindus settled in East and West Pakistan were being brutally killed and looted, the Congress, because of its soft-spoken nature, could neither speak against it nor do anything to mitigate the sufferings of the troubled people. It was then that Dr Shyama Prasad Mukherjee stood up and informed the Congress about the atrocities being committed on Hindus and asked the Congress to take steps for the safe passage of Hindus. He was the commerce minister in the first ministry constituted on 15 August 1947. He laid the foundation of the aeroplane-manufacturing unit Hindustan Aeronautics Ltd. in Bangalore, Chittaranjan Rail Factory, fertiliser plant etc. But in 1950, he resigned from the post in protest against the atrocities being committed on Hindus in Pakistan. And from then on he worked for the protection of the rights of Hindus till his death. It was towards this end that he went to Jammu & Kashmir where he was placed under arrest in Kathua and denied all facilities. Even his son was denied permission to see him and he died on 24 June 1953.

Shyama Prasad Mukherjee's father, Sir Ashutosh Mukherjee, was a prominent personality of Bengal. When Shyama Prasad was born, Sir Ashutosh was the lifeline of Calcutta University. After completing his education, Shyama Prasad followed the footsteps of his father and joined public service. In 1934, he became the Vice-Chancellor of Calcutta University. In 1936, he was chosen from the University area as a member of the Bengal State Assembly. In 1941 Fazlul Haque constituted a Cabinet along with the Hindus and made Shyama Prasad Mukherjee the finance minister.

In 1942, Midnapur district of Bengal came under the grip of severe floods and there was heavy loss of life and property. But the British governor denied Shyama Prasad Mukherjee permission to tour the affected areas. So he resigned from the Cabinet. Then he mobilised support and took the help of the Mahabodhi Society, the Ramakrishna Mission and the Marwari Relief Society to organise relief for those affected by the floods. It was during those days that Dhaka became the centre of riots. Dr Mukherjee held talks with the Nawab of Dhaka and helped restore peace and normalcy. Dr Mukherjee was moved to see the plight of Hindu refugees who had come from Pakistan.

Dr Mukherjee was the president of the Mahabodhi Society. When the mortal remains of Lord Buddha were brought to India from England, they were handed over to Dr Mukherjee. He took the relics to Burma, Cambodia, Vietnam and Bangkok. Wherever he went, he was welcomed with open arms and the relics were worshipped. On his return to India, he placed the relics inside the Sanchi Stupa.

In 1951, along with leaders of the Rashtriya Swayamsevak Sangh (RSS), Dr Mukherjee founded the Bharatiya Jan Sangh (BJS). Even after his death the party continued to grow stronger and gave national leaders of the stature of Atal Behari Vajpayee. The BJS was the forerunner of the Bharatiya Janata Party (BJP).

Atal Behari Vajpayee

Former Prime Minister and Veteran Parliamentarian

(Born 1924)

The name Atal Behari Vajpayee evokes such warm feelings that every Indian holds him in high esteem. Whatever he does, he always upholds the nation's pride, honour and dignity.

Atal Behari Vajpayee was born into a Brahmin family on 25 December 1924, at Gwalior, Madhya Pradesh. His father was a school teacher. Vajpayee was educated at Gwalior and Kanpur. He was a student of political science – a subject that was to prepare him for the future. Atal Behari Vajpayee was inclined towards politics even as a teenager. He was imprisoned for a brief period during the British rule for his anti-British activities. As a youth, he was attracted towards communism, but because the communists supported the partition of the country and the creation of Pakistan, he was disillusioned. It was then that he was influenced by the Rashtriya Swayamsevak Sangh (RSS), an organisation that was formed to instil a sense of honour among Hindus. He gave up his studies and joined as an editor of a publication of the RSS. In 1957, he joined the Bharatiya Jan Sangh (BJS), a forerunner of the Bharatiya Janata Party (BJP), which he was to co-found later with other political stalwarts.

Atal Behari Vajpayee was first elected to the Lok Sabha in 1957. Since then he has been elected to the Lok Sabha seven times and twice to the Rajya Sabha. During the Emergency, he was jailed along with other prominent opposition leaders. In the Janata-led Government that was elected to power in 1977, he served as foreign minister and helped strengthen ties with China and Pakistan. In 1980, he became a co-founder of the Bharatiya Janata Party (BJP) which advocates Hindutva, the feeling of pride in Hindu culture and values. Its popularity can be judged by the fact that in the 1984 elections, the party won just two seats and in the 1991 elections, it arnered so much support that it won 117 seats in the Lok Sabha. The demolition of the Babri Masjid at Ayodhya in December 1992 by organisations associated with the party led to a major setback in the party's popularity. But Atal Behari Vajpayee was one of those few leaders who regretted the demolition and condemned the act.

In May 1996, Atal Behari Vajpayee was sworn in as the eleventh prime minister. But his term lasted only 13 days because he was not able to garner enough support from other parties. In the next parliamentary elections held in 1998, the BJP and its allies formed the government led by Atal Behari Vajpayee. However the All India Anna Dravida Munnetra Kazagham (AIADMK) withdrew its support to the BJP-led Government, leading to its fall. In this brief span, India conducted the Pokhran II tests in May 1998, as Vajpayee put it 'to serve as a deterrent against our neighbours', who were harbouring evil intentions against India. The whole operation was carried out under cover and even took the Americans by surprise. There was condemnation in the West and economic sanctions were imposed on India by the US, the UK, France and other Western countries. Vajpayee remained defiant and declared: "India had the sanction of her own past glory and future vision to become strong."

As no other party had enough support to stake a claim to form the government, the country went into yet another mid-term poll in 1999. This time the BJP formed an alliance called the National Democratic Alliance (NDA), which was a coalition of different national and regional parties. The alliance won and as the leader of the largest party in the alliance, Atal Behari Vajpayee became the prime minister for the third time. He is the second prime minister after Pt Jawaharlal Nehru to be sworn in thrice.

Atal Behari Vajpayee is not just a politician, he has written several books. His speeches made as minister of external affairs have been compiled as *New Dimensions of Foreign Policy*. He is also a well-known poet. Among his published poems is *Meri Ikkyavan Kavitayen* ("My Fifty-one Poems"). The NDA got a debacle in the Lok Sabha elections held in 2004.

Dr Zakir Hussain

Founder of Basic Education/
Former President of India

(1897–1969)

The inspiration behind Dr Zakir Hussain's dream of basic education was Gandhiji. The deep sense of respect and love that he had for Gandhiji can be judged by the following words he said soon after being elected the president:

"By choosing me the President, the country has honoured a teacher. About 47 years ago, I had pledged that I would dedicate a majority of my years to national education. I had started my social life under the guidance of Gandhiji. He inspired me and showed me the way. I have now been given a new chance to serve. I will strive to lead my people through the path shown by Gandhiji."

Dr Zakir Hussain was born on 8 February 1897 in Hyderabad. He took over as the President of India in 1967 after Dr S. Radhakrishnan. His appointment as the president reiterated that India is a secular country.

Dr Hussain was a teacher by profession. In 1937, when popular governments came up in the states, Gandhiji wanted that these governments should try to improve the level of education of their citizens. He wanted that children be given an education that would help in their mental and physical growth. Gandhiji was against the idea that education should be restricted within the school syllabus. He wanted the children to get educated through practical lessons rather than theory. This is what he called fundamental education. So he formed a committee. The work of the committee was to formulate a syllabus for basic education.

Dr Hussain made the report with great dedication. The report received lavish praise. This report was different from conventional ones. Gandhiji also liked the report and supported Dr Hussain. He was impressed by Dr Hussain's capability. So Gandhiji formed the Hindustani Talimi Sangh (National Committee on Basic Education) in 1937 that was to work on the lines of Dr Hussain's report. Dr Hussain was appointed the chairman of the committee.

Dr Hussain was a descendant of the Afridi Pathans of Afghanistan. Some families of the tribe had migrated to India and settled in the Farrokhabad district of Uttar Pradesh. A majority of the people were soldiers and some were also landowners and farmers. One of the families of the tribe was that of Fida Hussain into which was born Zakir Hussain. Fida Hussain left for Hyderabad and started practising law. Zakir Hussain's early education took place in Hyderabad.

After the death of his parents, he went to Itawa to seek education and there he came in contact with a Sufi saint. This chance meeting evoked a sense of respect for every religion in the mind of young Hussain. After finishing matriculation, he went to Aligarh for further studies. It was when he was studying MA that Mahatma Gandhi beckoned students to leave State-supported institutions. Dr Zakir Hussain left college and laid the foundation of Jamia Millia Islamia (JMI). He worked in JMI for a few years and then went to Germany for further studies. He obtained a doctorate in economics from Berlin University.

After returning from Germany, he worked to improve the condition of JMI at the behest of Gandhiji and Pt Nehru. JMI shifted base from Aligarh to Delhi. He remained Vice-Chancellor of JMI for 22 years. During his years at Aligarh, he displayed such simplicity, austerity and economy that he did not have any peon or clerk to help him out with the office work. He carried out all the work himself because the financial condition of JMI was not good. At first he drew a salary of Rs 300 per month, but when he saw that JMI could not bear this expense, he himself made a cut in his salary and worked at Rs 150 per month. During his tenure at JMI, he displayed his sacrificial spirit and selflessness and did not let the institution become a centre of communal politics.

Whatever work Dr Hussain did, he left his indelible mark on it. In 1948, Dr Hussain became the Vice-Chancellor of Aligarh Muslim University. In 1952, he entered the Rajya Sabha. In 1957, when he was made the Governor of Bihar, he won the hearts of the people by his sympathy, wit, discipline and extrovert nature. In 1956-58 he served on the executive board of the United Nations Educational, Scientific and Cultural Organisation (UNESCO). Between 1962 and 1967, he served as the Vice President of India and the Chairman of the Rajya Sabha. He never discriminated between the ruling party or the opposition, nor did he let the ruling party take any advantage. After the fourth general elections when the presidential candidate was to be chosen, everyone believed that the obvious choice would be Dr Zakir Hussain. However, due to opposition the candidate had to be chosen through the ballot. But Dr Zakir Hussain emerged a clear winner. On 13 May 1967, he was appointed the President of India. The world, particularly Germany, welcomed his presidency.

Dr Hussain had a great sense of humour and had the knack of getting work done from his colleagues. Once a child had come to school wearing a dirty cap. He washed the cap for the child and taught the child a lesson in cleanliness. Once some windowpanes were so dirty that they could not be cleaned, so he broke them. He had a servant who had the habit of getting up late in the morning. One day, Dr Hussain threw a bucket of water over him and said, "Sir, have your bath. The water is ready. I have brought your morning tea. Do wake up or it will turn cold." From that day onwards, the servant used to always get up on time.

Dr Zakir Hussain loved flowers, different types of stones, jewellery and paintings. Dr Hussain also wrote a few books. In recognition of Zakir Hussain's contributions, he was conferred the Bharat Ratna in 1963.

Dr Zakir Hussain died on 3 May 1969, the first Indian President to die in office. He is buried on the campus of the Jamia Millia Islamia (a central University) in New Delhi.

Rajiv Gandhi

The Youngest Prime Minister of India

(1944–1991)

When Rajiv Gandhi became the Prime Minister of India, everyone said that he would not be able to hold the reigns of the government for long because he was inexperienced. But what they forgot was that he was born into the Nehru-Gandhi family, which was politically involved with the freedom struggle and later in nation building. So Rajiv Gandhi inherited the political legacy of the Nehru-Gandhi family from Pt Motilal Nehru, Pt Jawaharlal Nehru, Indira Gandhi and Feroze Gandhi. Rajiv Gandhi was young, dynamic and a man with foresight. It is only because of his sincere endeavour that the country is today a leading name in the I.T. revolution and mass communication.

Rajiv Gandhi was the youngest Prime Minister of India. In 1984, after the assassination of his mother Indira Gandhi, Rajiv Gandhi became the prime minister. His brother, Sanjay, had earlier died in a plane crash. Sanjay Gandhi was politically inclined from the start but Rajiv Gandhi was not. Rajiv Gandhi studied in a public school in Dehradun and later in England. Rajiv was trained as a pilot and joined the Indian Airlines. While in England, Rajiv met Sonia, an Italian citizen, whom he married later. Both were happy in their household when tragedy struck the Gandhi family. Sanjay Gandhi died in a plane crash in 1980. Sanjay was being groomed as Indira Gandhi's political heir. It was then that she decided to take Rajiv under her wing and groom him as her political heir. In spite of protests from Sonia, Rajiv joined the political arena and began to assist his mother.

In October 1984, Indira Gandhi was assassinated by her own security guards. Rajiv Gandhi was sworn in as the prime minister. In the general elections that followed, the Congress emerged the clear winner with a huge majority. And Rajiv Gandhi was sworn in as the prime minister. The people had high hopes from their young leader and he also won the respect and admiration of world leaders. However, on the home front, the opposition began to harp on the issue of Bofors and this resulted in his growing unpopularity. So in the 1989 elections, the Congress was defeated.

V.P. Singh was sworn in as the Prime Minister of India. He was the leader of the Janata Dal. The implementation of the Mandal Commission report during his tenure soon made him unpopular and he was forced to resign after losing a no-confidence motion. Chandra Shekhar took over, but the Janata Dal could not complete its five-year term. The 15-month-old ninth Lok Sabha was dissolved and fresh general elections were announced.

The nation's allegience shifted towards Rajiv Gandhi and the Congress. They wanted a stable government that would last its full term in office. Rajiv Gandhi went on a whirlwind tour of the nation to ensure the vote of the masses. However, on 21 May 1991, Rajiv was assassinated by a lady suicide bomber of the LTTE at Sriperumbudur in Tamil Nadu.

On 17 June 1991, he was posthumously awarded the Bharat Ratna. The Congress legacy is now being carried on by Sonia Gandhi and their charismatic son Rahul.

Dr Ram Manohar Lohia

Socialist Leader

(1910–1967)

Dr Ram Manohar Lohia's name is reckoned amongst the greatest Indian thinkers of the past Century. He was one of the first to foster the socialist ideology and work towards its cause. If we analyse his thoughts in retrospect, we will realise that he was basically advocating extremist thoughts. But this gentleman was born in an era when extremist thoughts were looked down upon.

Most Indians consider themselves god-fearing and do not think it proper to foster extremist thoughts. But Lohia believed that if we as responsible men and women did nothing for the oppressed classes, then talking about god was in vain.

On one hand, Lohia was a champion of democratic thought and a good orator on India's democratic principles. On the other, he gave it the form of a revolution and kindled its flame in the hearts of millions of Indians. Communist ideology was a part of that revolution which believed that casteism and religious fundamentalism were handicaps to the progress of a country and damaging to society. He believed that it was because of these wrong ideologies that mankind was losing its compassion. His speeches about this subject were full of passion. He had also penned down most of his thoughts. Just as he was against casteism, he also firmly opposed socialist dogmas.

He also opposed the principles of the Congress, although in the beginning he was associated with the Congress. But he soon felt that the ideology of the Congress was a hindrance to the progress of the nation. So he left the Congress and tried to steer the country towards communist ideology.

It is believed that the ancestors of Dr Ram Manohar Lohia

traded in iron and so took the name 'Lohia'. Ram Manohar was born in Ayodhya. His mother died when he was very young. His father, Hiralal Lohia, was a firm believer in the ideology of the Congress. When the Simon Commission came to India, Ram Manohar Lohia was pursuing his education at Calcutta University. He led the students of Calcutta. After completing his education, Lohia received a scholarship and went to Germany to conduct research in Economics. After his return he joined the Congress Socialist Party. For some time, he edited the party's weekly newsletter *Congress Socialist*. He actively participated in the country's freedom struggle and went to jail several times. In 1948, he resigned from the Congress and joined the Communist Party. He was chosen chief secretary of the party.

Dr Lohia was a powerful orator. His style of delivering speeches was utterly original. When he was a Member of Parliament, Pt Nehru respected his policies and ideology. Whether Dr Lohia made speeches inside the Parliament or outside, the audience would listen to him spellbound, and there would be pindrop silence in the hall. Almost all the top Congress leaders feared confrontation with him. He led an extremely simple and austere life. So people called him a "political sage".

One of the most loved leaders of the past Century's intellectual class died on 12 October 1967, but his revolutionary thinking continues to inspire people.

Jyoti Basu

Chief Minister with a Record Tenure

(1914-2010)

What made Jyoti Basu special is the fact that despite owing allegiance to the Communist Party (Marxist), he was elected democratically to become the longest reigning chief minister. He was elected to the position when he was 63 and held on to it till 86. He gave up his position only in the year 2000 due to failing health.

When the Communist Party first came to power, a majority of the people did not have any experience in running the state's affairs. But it was because of Jyoti Basu's political acumen, discernment and wisdom that he could hold on to his position by getting elected five times consecutively. His party CPI(M) had run the West Bengal Government under the leadership of B. Bhattacharya till middle of 2011 when Mamta Banerjee of Trinamool Congress took over the reigns.

The reason behind Jyoti Basu's immense popularity was that his government always cared for the cause of farmers and workers.

In the 1977 general and state elections, the Congress faced a terrible defeat in the Lok Sabha and the State Assembly elections. Even in West Bengal, the Congress was routed. The void left by the Congress in the political arena of West Bengal was filled by the Communist Party (Marxist) under the able leadership of Jyoti Basu.

Jyoti Basu studied in St. Xavier's School and Presidency College. Then he went to England to study law. There he came in contact with Harold Lasky, a renowned communist leader. Among Jyoti Basu's close associates were Rajni Patel, Mohan Kumaramangalam, Renu Chakravarti, Nikhil Chakravarti and Arun Bose.

Jyoti Basu had joined the Indian Communist Party at a time when the British Government had declared it illegal. In 1964, Jyoti Basu formed the Communist Party (Marxist). He was a member of the Central Committee and the Politburo right from the beginning. Under his successful administration the state of Bengal took great strides.

Jyoti Basu served as the Chief Minister of West Bengal from 1977 to 2000, making him the longest serving Chief Minister of any Indian State. He had remained a member of the CPI(M) Politburo from the time of party's founding in 1964 until 2008. Thereafter, until his death in 2010, he remained a permanent invitee to the Central Committee of CPI(M).

On 17 January 2010, Jyoti Basu breathed his last in a Kolkata hospital following pneumonia and multiple organ failure.

Chandrababu Naidu

The IT-savvy CM of Andhra Pradesh

(Born 1951)

Andhra Pradesh has produced many eminent people who have contributed a lot for the progress of the state, yet it is plagued by many problems. Some parts of Andhra Pradesh are backward and infested by Naxalites. Some of these problems came down to Chandrababu Naidu as a legacy, while many were created during his tenure. What is significant about Chandrababu Naidu is that he transformed the Nizam's old city into such an amazing world of Information Technology that his work finds mention not only in India, but also abroad. This was proved from the fact that the then President of America, Bill Clinton, included the city in his itinerary when he visited the country and praised Chandrababu Naidu for his work.

Apart from carrying out wonderful work in the field of Information Technology, he consolidated the position of his party, Telugu Desam, by joining hands with the National Democratic Alliance (NDA) and helping Atal Behari Vajpayee in forming a strong government at the Centre. Both at the national and the state level, he has displayed prudence and stability. He gave his full allegiance to the government, but also remained loyal to his state. It is because of this reason that he did not support those decisions of the Centre which could be harmful for his state or its people.

Chandrababu Naidu was born in a poor farmer's family in Chittoor district of Andhra Pradesh. He was inclined towards politics even in his youth, so before finishing his education, he joined the Congress. But seeing the zeal of this youth, Telugu Desam leader NT Rama Rao inducted him into his party and appointed him the general secretary. NT Rama Rao gave his daughter in marriage to Chandrababu Naidu. But after NTR's death, when his second wife Laxmi Parvati tried to usurp power, Naidu intervened and took over the reigns of the party. He became the Chief Minister of the state in September 1995.

Chandrababu Naidu has the same beliefs as Atal Behari Vajpayee over the success of a coalition government. His Telugu Desam Party played a key role in the formation of the government at the Centre. Naidu is one of the few chief ministers who has worked to put his state on the path of progress. He is also fully aware of the primary necessities of the people of his state.

Chandrababu Naidu is a man with foresight. In a very short time, he has etched his name in the list of prominent personalities of the 20th Century. He was defeated by Congress in May 2004 assembly elections.

Bidhan Chandra Roy

The Founder of Modern Bengal

(1882-1962)

Apart from the contribution of barristers and lawyers in the freedom struggle, many doctors also participated and prominent among them was Dr Bidhan Chandra Roy. Although Dr Ghosh was appointed the first Chief Minister of Bengal after Independence, the public wanted Dr Roy to occupy the position. The reason was that after Partition, Bengal suffered immensely and people believed that only Dr Roy could restore normalcy and put the state on the path to progress. When Dr Roy was appointed the chief minister, he did not spare any efforts to transform the state. He established the Durgapur Steel Factory, Chittaranjan Rail Factory and the Damodar Valley Corporation.

Dr Bidhan Chandra Roy was the descendant of King Pratapaditya, a legendary figure of Bengal. All his life Pratapaditya displayed valour and fought against the Mughals. But his army was no match against the army of Jehangir and he was captured. When he was being taken to be presented before the court of Jehangir, he killed himself rather than face disgrace.

The opulence of the family had been drained during his father's time itself, so Dr Roy had to face a lot of difficulties in his education. After completing his B.A. from Patna, he went to Calcutta to study medicine at the Medical College. Then he went to England and received the degrees of MRCP and FRCS. After that he worked in the regional health services.

While in Calcutta University, Dr Roy was closely associated with the famous leader Sir Ashutosh Mukherjee. So when the latter founded the Carmichael Medical College, he invited Dr Roy to join the institution. Dr Roy left his job and joined the college in 1919 and remained associated with it till the end.

When he became the chief minister, he did not resign from it, but took leave.

Sir Ashutosh was the inspiration behind Dr Roy's entry into politics. When the elections were held in 1923, Dr Roy stood for the first time from Calcutta (N) area. Sir Surendranath Banerjee was his opponent. Dr Roy defeated him by 3,500 votes.

Then it became difficult for him to separate himself from the Congress. In 1931, he was elected the Mayor of Calcutta. He had by then become a national leader. In the Congress Session held in Calcutta in 1926, he was elected Minister of the Committee. The satyagraha movement in Bengal was led by Dr Roy. In 1934, he was elected the president of the Bengal Congress.

West Bengal will never be able to forget the contributions of Dr Bidhan Chandra Roy. He died in July 1962 at the age of 80.

Dr Bidhan Chandra Roy was awarded Bharat Ratna in the year 1961.

Social Reformers

Maharishi Karve

Social Reformer

(1858–1962)

Maharishi Dhondu Keshav Karve not only gave a new lease of life to innumerable widows, but also started a revolution for women's education and upliftment in the whole of Maharashtra.

Maharishi Karve was born on 18 April 1858 in a small village, Sheravali, of Konkan district. He had special interest in education, but getting an education was difficult in those days.

At the age of 15, he was married to 9-year-old Radhabai. At the age of 23, he passed his matric from Mumbai. Four years later, he graduated from Elphinston College. Unlike other young people of his age, he did not want to serve the British Government, so he decided to take up teaching as a profession. Around this time, he was devastated by the news of his wife's death in the village. At the same time, Gopal Krishna Gokhale invited him to join Ferguson College in Poona, as professor of mathematics. He soon became the most admired teacher of his college.

Leading a single life soon made him feel the need for a companion. When the talk of a second marriage came up, he expressed the desire to marry a widow. The British Government had then officially declared remarriage of widows as legal. However, society did not permit the remarriage of widows. Ramabai, a prominent reformist, had started a centre called *Sharda Sadan* to educate widows. It was here that the younger sister of one of Karve's friends, Narhari Pant, was seeking education. The young widow was Godavari. She was married at the age of eight and three months later she had become a child widow. On 13 March 1893 Karve married Godavari at the residence of Dr Ambedkar Bhandarkar, a famous scholar. The bride was given a new name – Anandibai.

The marriage was solemnised, but society did not accept it and boycotted him. He rallied the thinkers of Poona to garner support and went from village to village to campaign for the cause of widows. In 1896, at a village named Hingne, he started a home for young orphan girls in a hut. Land was allocated for the home and funds poured in. Now a permanent home stands in place of the hut.

When Maharishi Karve came across a Japanese journal, he realised that there were universities meant for women. So he decided to start a similar university in India. He left Ferguson College and totally dedicated himself to the setting up of such a university. Sir Vithaldas Thackersay, a famous industrialist, donated Rs 15 lakhs for the university in memory of his mother.

This donation helped speed up the project. In 1920, the university, Maharishi Karve Stree Shikshan Sanstha, was formally inaugurated. Karve also went to foreign countries to garner funds for the university. His wife Anandibai stood steadfast by his side.

After Independence, the university was recognised by the government. In 1958, he was awarded the Bharat Ratna. He died on 9 November 1962, at the grand old age of 105 years.

Baba Amte

Social Activist

(1914–2008)

It is difficult to put Baba Amte into the category of a saint or a social activist or even as a combination of the two. Baba Amte was only one of his kind, so it is all the more difficult to compare him with anyone else in the world. Baba Amte's spirit of sacrifice and service was so high that he often forgot his own worries and strives for the betterment of the underprivileged and the needy.

Despite suffering from cervical spondylitis that made it difficult for him to sit and stand straight, he worked for the welfare of leprosy patients, who are usually looked down upon by society. Most people are unaware that the disease is now curable, so whenever they see a leper, a feeling of aversion or sympathy is evoked in them. Most parts of the body of the victims like fingers, toes, ears and nose are reduced to stubs, after a period of time, because of the disease. Yet Baba Amte cared for them.

Apart from this, he was involved in other social activities too. He carried just a mat and a walking stick with him. Besides these personal belongings, he wore just two pieces of clothing – a pair of shorts spun out of Khadi and a sleeveless vest.

Former President K.R. Narayanan had honoured him with the 'Gandhi Peace Prize' that included prize money of Rs 1 crore. He spent the entire sum on the social uplift of the downtrodden.

Baba Amte was born Murlidhar Devidas Amte in Hinganghat, Wardha district, Maharashtra on 24 December 1914 into a family of *jagirdars* (landowners). Even as a child, Baba Amte was compassionate towards his servants and the lower classes. He studied law and set up practice in Wardha, which soon flourished. In 1942, when the nation responded to the call of Gandhiji and many prominent leaders were imprisoned, he organised lawyers to plead cases of imprisoned leaders. He was arrested. It was around this time that he saw a leper in Warora and that changed the course of his life. He gave up his profession and began to work for the uplift of lepers and the downtrodden.

In 1949, Baba Amte founded Anandvan for the rehabilitation of lepers who were shunned by society. The sprawling 50 acres of barren land soon became a self-sufficient centre with its own university, hospital, technical units, orphanage, dairy and farmlands.

In the 1980s, Baba Amte launched two *Bharat Jodo* movements to promote national integration. In 1985, he went on a tour from Kashmir to Kanyakumari. In 1988, he undertook a tour from Assam to Gujarat. In 1989, he established the ashram called Nijibal ("inner strength"), as a mark of protest against the construction of the Sardar Sarovar Dam in the Narmada Valley and the resultant displacement of tribals from the area.

For his humanitarian work, he was honoured with the Padma Shri in 1971, the Rashtriya Bhushan in 1978, the Padma Vibhushan in 1986 and the Magsaysay Award in 1988.

Due to his health problems during the last 15 years of his life, most of the work was handled by his son, Prakash Amte.

In 2007, he was diagnosed with leukemia. Baba Amte died in Anandvan on 9 February 2008. Respecting his wishes, his body was buried instead of being cremated, the traditional funeral of Hindus.

Baba Amte is remembered for his contribution towards rehabilitation and empowerment of poor people suffering from leprosy.

Vinoba Bhave

Founder of the Bhoodan Movement

(1895–1982)

A charya Vinoba Bhave not only remained away from politics, he also remained away from publicity. Not only that, he remained detached from all the major events that rocked India and had even given up reading newspapers. So what were the character traits that make him an eminent personality? The significance of his work can be estimated from the fact that although India is an agriculture-based country, the majority of farmers do not even have a patch of land to call their own. Vinoba Bhave's attention was drawn towards this problem and he went on a campaign to ask big farmers to contribute land for landless farmers – a revolution that was named *Bhoodan* – gift of land. He collected land from landlords and gave it away to landless farmers.

It all began one day when he was touring the villages of Andhra Pradesh to appeal for land for Harijans (low-caste Hindus) and a landholder offered him a part of his land. It was then that the idea of the land-gift movement was conceived. Vinobaji held prayer meetings like Gandhiji. So that evening, after the prayer meeting, Vinobaji put forward a request for 80 acres of land from the people of the village. Such was the influence of Vinobaji's words that one of the wealthiest farmers of the village donated not 80, but 100 acres of land. And this was how the Bhoodan Movement began.

Working on Gandhiji's principle of *ahimsa*, or non-violence, he went from village to village appealing for the gift of land from wealthy landowners. He believed that land reform could be secured not by government action, but by the change of heart of the people. Then he went on a *padyatra* (walking tour), across the nation for collecting more land. He went to Bihar and sought the help of Jayprakash Narayan (JP). Bihar had a lot of wealthy landlords. With the help of JP, Vinobaji was able to collect hundreds of acres of land. He toured the country for some 14 years. He visited 45,000 villages and met millions of people and collected about 1,70,000 hectares of land, which he donated to poor farmers.

There have been examples in history where great men had to face troubles on their path towards progress. Vinobaji also had his share of trials and tribulations. His ambition was not just to provide poor Harijans with land but to elevate their financial and social status. So wherever he went, he tried to help Harijans get back into mainstream India and be accepted in society. Thus, he wanted them to be allowed into temples and in many places he faced resentment due to this.

During his *padyatra*, he also established many ashrams. His work was similar to that of Shankaracharya. As heir to Gandhiji's legacy, Vinobaji not only kept alive spiritualism but took it further and gave it a new direction.

His critics claimed that through the Bhoodan Movement, Vinobaji was encouraging the fragmentation of land and thus hindering the growth of large-scale agriculture. Later, he encouraged *gramdan*, where villagers pooled their land and worked as a co-operative.

Vinayak Narahari Vinoba was born on 11 September 1895 in Gagode, Gujarat into a high-caste Chitpavan Brahmin family. His father Narahari and mother Rukmani Devi were extremely religious people. While doing household chores, his mother chanted bhajans sung by Marathi saints. She called him Vinay. Little did she realise that her son would grow up to be a true replica of *vinay* – humility. Even as a young child, Vinobaji was unlike his peers. After his early education he passed his matric in 1913 from Baroda and took admission in Intermediate. He was able to learn by heart anything that he read for the first time. He read books on religion, literature and history from the famous library of Baroda. He was also interested in mathematics. In 1916 he gave up his studies to join Gandhiji's ashram.

One day, while sitting with his mother in the kitchen, he burnt all his certificates. When his mother asked him the reason, he replied that he did not require them, as his direction in life was different. Then he went to Kashi and studied Sanskrit. It was around this time that Madan Mohan Malaviya had established the Kashi Hindu University. Malaviya invited Gandhiji to the institution. Gandhiji had just returned from South Africa. Gandhiji inaugurated the University and gave an inaugural speech. When Vinoba read the text of the speech in the newspapers the next day, he began to yearn to see Gandhiji in person.

He went to meet Gandhiji at an ashram in Kochrab. As per Gandhiji's wishes, Vinobaji took charge of the old age home at Sabarmati. The meditation, penance and study he did during the period, put him in the category of learned men. Apart from looking after the home, he was actively involved in the other constructive works of Gandhiji, like the manufacture of Khadi, basic education, cleanliness, etc. He stayed there till 1932 and then moved over to a colony of Harijans at Nalwadi, a village that was a few kilometres away from Wardha.

Between the 1920s and 1940s he went to prison several times. In fact, he was imprisoned for five years in the 1940s for leading non-violent resistance against British rule.

He had resolved to survive on the money received from spinning his own yarn. But it was difficult to sustain oneself on this money. Lack of proper diet made him sick. Gandhiji advised him to go to a hill station, but Vinobaji went to stay at the hill of a village near river Pavnar. This helped him recover and he made Pavnar Ashram the centre of his activities.

Vinobaji participated in the satyagraha movements of Gandhiji. In the Nagpur Flag Satyagraha of 1923, he was imprisoned for 12 months. After returning from the Round Table Conference, Gandhiji was arrested in Bombay. Later Vinobaji was also put in prison. During his sentence, at the behest of fellow freedom fighters, he began to give discourses from the *Bhagavad Gita*. These discourses have been published in Hindi, English and about 20 other languages.

The fame of Vinobaji spread across the nation in 1940 during the Second World War, when India was dragged into the War without the consent of Indian leaders. During the satyagraha in 1940, Gandhiji chose Vinobaji as his worthy successor. In October, he was sent to prison. In 1942, during the Quit India Movement, he was again arrested. After the sentence, he returned to Pavnar Ashram and took over the work of village welfare. After Partition, he toured the nation to alleviate the pain of riot victims and to rehabilitate Harijans. The *Bhoodan Yojna*, published in 1953, is a series of articles that explain his philosophy of life and the movement that he started.

After Independence and the death of Gandhiji, the nation began to see him as a saint and social activist. A number of leaders and ministers consulted Vinobaji regarding spiritual and social aspects of life and political dilemmas. In 1975, he maintained a vow of silence over the issue of the involvement of his followers in the political agitation. He was thus able to persuade the government to enforce a law prohibiting the killing of cows throughout India. Cows are considered sacred by Hindus.

In spite of all these achievements, Vinobaji felt that he no longer had any special role to play, so he gave up food. On 14 November 1982, his condition deteriorated. He had also given up drinking water. The next day he died.

In 1983, he was awarded the Bharat Ratna posthumously.

Ela Bhatt

Champion of Women's Empowerment

(Born 1933)

As the economic position of women in Indian society is entirely dependent on their menfolk, their predicament is pitiable. In many states, it has been observed that in spite of working more than men, women have to depend on the men for survival.

Today efforts are being undertaken to improve the socio-economic position of women and to give them equal rights as men. The contribution made by Ela Bhatt towards the elevation of women at the grassroots level is commendable. She founded SEWA (Self-Employed Women's Association), a trade union of poor, self-employed women working in the unorganised sector. The institution has branches in all major cities of India. It provides training to women to make them self-reliant enough to look after their families. SEWA also provides assistance to backward and down-trodden sections of society. They are provided education so that they can make their lives worthwhile.

Impressed by the work of the SEWA, UNICEF and other wings of the United Nations Organisation have provided financial assistance to the organisation. Other international organisations also provide assistance to SEWA.

SEWA helps down-trodden women in finding access to the basic necessities so that they are not dependent on men. SEWA provides assistance to working women of the labour class to liberate them from the clutches of trade unions, which are dominated by men.

Ela Bhatt studied law and joined the Textile Labour Association started by Gandhiji. She strived to bring together all women working in the unorganised sector. Towards this effort, she established SEWA in 1972. Today SEWA has around 200,000 members. In 1974, she started SEWA Cooperative Bank with the aim of providing small loans to poor, down-trodden women to help them start their own earning activity. In the late 1990s, the bank had 60,000 members. Apart from its regular services, the bank also offers legal advice.

In 1986, Ela Bhatt was nominated to the Rajya Sabha. When she took over as the chairperson of the National Commission on Self-Employed Women, she drew the attention of the government towards the plight of poor women working in unorganised sectors.

For her indepth knowledge on various issues that plague society and poor women in particular, Ela Bhatt's advice is sought worldwide in matters related to banking, gender studies, policy-making and anti-poverty programmes. She was a member of the Consultative Group to Assist the Poorest of the World Bank. Between 1984 and 1988 she was the chairperson of the New York-based Women's World Banking.

Ela Bhatt has been bestowed several national and international honorary degrees and won many national and international awards. In recognition of her contribution to society, she received the Ramon Magsaysay Award for Community Leadership in 1977. In 1984, she received the Right Livelihood Award (the Alternative Nobel Prize) for "Changing the Human Environment". She was awarded the Padma Shri in 1985 and the Padma Bhushan in 1986.

Mother Teresa

Messiah of the Poor

(1910–1997)

Although Mother Teresa was born in a foreign country, her area of work was in India. She dedicated her life in the service of the 'poorest of the poor'. Mother Teresa was a Yugoslavian, but she chose India as the base of her humanitarian work, which soon spread to other countries.

Mother Teresa was born Agnes Gonxha Bojaxhiu in Skopje, Yugoslavia on 27 August 1910. By the age of 12, it was clear that she intended to become a nun. In 1928, at the age of 18, she joined the Order of Loreto nuns at a town in Ireland. Six weeks later, in 1929, she sailed to India to join a Loreto school in Calcutta (now Kolkata) as a teacher.

On 10 September 1946, when she was making a railway journey to Darjeeling, she heard the 'Voice of God' from within. She received the message that she had to dedicate her life towards the service of the poor of Calcutta. She said, "The message was clear, but I had to wait for permission from the Pope to be released from the Loreto Order and to start on my own."

After obtaining the Pope's permission, she left the Order. She gave up the black and white dress of the Order and wore a coarse blue-bordered saree. In 1948 Sister Teresa became Mother Teresa. She also became an Indian citizen. She studied nursing before moving to the slums. The plight of the poor in Calcutta could make anyone shudder. They lived in abject poverty and led miserable lives because of lack of food, clean water and medical care. The women, the aged and young children needed attention the most. Along with the poor, there were lepers who were looked down upon by society.

She founded the Missionaries of Charity in 1948 in a pilgrim hostel near the sacred Kali temple. The premises were given to her by the municipal authorities. The organisation received pontifical sanction from Pope Pius XII and formally began work in 1950. In 1965 the Order became a pontifical congregation.

Initially, money and aid were scarce. But that didn't deter her. Seeing her work, aid soon followed. She herself went out on the roads of Calcutta and picked up hapless people. The first woman she picked up was half eaten by rats and ants. But she could not be saved. She died in Mother's arms and that strengthened her resolve to dedicate her life to the cause of the poor.

Then she started Nirmal Hriday (Place of the Pure Heart) in the empty halls given to her by the Calcutta Corporation. Nirmal Hriday grew into 62 centres across the country. The home looked after the poor and the dying. "Nobody there has died feeling unwanted or unloved. We help the poor to die in peace."

Mother was also moved by the plight of lepers. Disowned by their own families, they were forced to beg on the streets. But even the people looked down upon them. This made her establish a home for lepers called Prem Niwas (Home of Love). "Touch a leper, touch him with love," said Mother. She built a leper colony near Asansol called Shanti Nagar (Town of Peace). She explained to the lepers that leprosy was a curable disease and that if they took care of themselves, there would be some improvement in their condition. In Titagarh, she founded the Mahatma Gandhi Leprosy Ashram. She herself brought many of those who suffered from the disease to the ashram.

Besides, Mother was also moved by the plight of newborn or the unborn, who were either abandoned after birth or killed before birth. So she established Nirmal Shishu Bhavan for poor, orphaned and abandoned children. Infants are brought to the home and looked after and nursed by the sisters. As they grow, the children are educated and trained for a profession.

Mother Teresa started her work with just Rs 5. Now the work has expanded to 750 centres in 125 countries. The centres provide education, medical facilities and a home for the poor, destitute and dying. At these centres, everyday around five lakh people are fed and clothed. The centres provide medical relief to about 1.5 lakh sick people and education to more than 20,000 children from slums and poor settlements. Besides, the centres also provide succour to people suffering from AIDS and substance abuse. Mother believed, "to do something beautiful for God is what life is all about".

Through her unflagging work, she commanded universal respect. It was thanks to this respect that she received government and private donations to carry out her work.

In 1964 when Pope Paul VI came to India and presented her with his ceremonial limousine, she immediately raffled it to raise money for her leper colony. In January 1971 she was honoured with the first Pope John XXIII Peace Prize by Pope Paul. The cash award of $21,500 went to the cause of leprosy patients. The cash money that came with the Magsaysay Award went into the construction of a children's home in Agra.

Mother Teresa was a simple lady. She always wore a white saree and had simple living and eating habits. She was awarded the Padma Shri in 1963 and the Nobel Peace Prize in 1979. She was also honoured with the Bharat Ratna, the Leo Tolstoy International Award, the British Order of Merit, the Ceres Medal of the FAO, apart from various other awards, but she claimed that her biggest honour was to work for the poor and the needy. She showed the world that if one had the 'milk of human kindness', one could see God in every human being.

On 5 September 1997 she died in Calcutta. The world mourned her death. India's "saint of the gutters" was buried in the Mother House, the headquarters of the Order of Missionaries of Charity.

Mother once said, "My work is just a drop when what is needed is an ocean of compassion. If I did not put in that one drop, the ocean would be one drop less." But it was French President Jacques Chirac who aptly summed up her contribution: "This evening there is less love, less compassion, less light in the world."

Dr B.R. Ambedkar

Leader of the Dalits

(1891–1956)

Dr Bhimrao Ramji Ambedkar was born into a low caste Mahar family on 14 April 1891 in Mhow, Madhya Pradesh. As society followed a rigid caste system, people of a low caste were considered untouchables. People of the Mahar caste were brave and admitted into the army. Bhimrao's father Ramji Rao also served in the army. When the family migrated to Bombay from their village, Bhimrao was admitted to Elphinston College. They lived in a small tenement where there was not enough space for the whole family, so the father and son slept in turns.

Ambedkar had to face a lot of difficulties in his quest for education. The Maharaja of Baroda helped him and so, after completing his B.A., he went to America for his Master's. He did research on India's economy and obtained his doctorate. After coming back to India, he started practising law in Bombay. Along with his practice, he also worked for the uplift of the socially backward classes. It was this work which drew him close to Gandhiji.

In 1931 when Gandhiji went to London for the Round Table Conference, he accompanied Gandhiji as a representative of the backward classes, while Gandhiji was the representative of the Congress. The Congress was not in favour of giving separate representation to the backward classes. But Ambedkar strongly advocated separate representation for the backward classes. A compromise was reached by the Poona Pact of 1932. The backward classes were given the right to draw water from local wells and ponds and visit temples and other public places. Due to the efforts of Dr Ambedkar, the attitude of society towards these classes changed. But Dr Ambedkar was not happy with the results, so he converted to Buddhism on 14 October 1956.

Ambedkar was accused of creating a rift in Hinduism when he converted to Buddhism. Earlier he had founded the Depressed Classes Association and worked for the amelioration of the suffering of the Dalits or backward classes. In 1947, Pt Nehru included him in his Cabinet as the law minister.

Ambedkar's health deteriorated because of his rigorous work. His wife had died many years ago. In 1948, at the age of 57, he married Lakshmi Savita. She was a doctor and took good care of Ambedkar. He died on 6 December 1956.

In 1990, the man who was the driving force behind the drafting of the Constitution of independent India, Dr Ambedkar was awarded the Bharat Ratna posthumously.

www.ingramcontent.com/pod-product-compliance
Lightning Source LLC
LaVergne TN
LVHW021616080426
835510LV00019B/2594